40 Shoi

DEVON

Dear Daddy

To keep you busy
in your retirement!

Happy Birthday

Love

Lucy

x x

Produced by AA Publishing
© AA Media Limited 2011

Researched and written by
Sue Viccars

Commissioning Editor: David Popey
Series Management: Sandy Draper
Series Design: Tracey Butler
Copy-editor: Pam Stagg
Proofreader: Chris Bagshaw
Picture Researcher: Michelle Aylott
Internal Repro and Image Manipulation:
Sarah Montgomery
Cartography provided by the Mapping
Services Department of AA Publishing
Production: Lorraine Taylor

Published by AA Publishing (a trading name
of AA Media Limited, whose registered office
is Fanum House, Basing View, Basingstoke,
Hampshire RG21 4EA; registered number
06112600)

  This product
includes mapping
data licensed from the Ordnance Survey®
with the permission of the Controller of
Her Majesty's Stationery Office. © Crown
Copyright 2011. All rights reserved.
Licence number 100021153.

A04616

978-0-7495-6902-0
978-0-7495-6914-3 (SS)

Colour separation by AA Digital

Printed by Oriental Press

Visit AA Publishing at theAA.com/shop

A CIP catalogue record for this book is
available from the British Library.

The contents of this book are believed
correct at the time of printing. Nevertheless,
the publishers cannot be held responsible
for any errors or omissions or for changes
in the details given in this book or for
the consequences of any reliance on the
information it provides. This does not affect
your statutory rights. We have tried to
ensure accuracy in this book, but things do
change and we would be grateful if readers
would advise us of any inaccuracies they
may encounter.

We have taken all reasonable steps to ensure
that these walks are safe and achievable
by walkers with a realistic level of fitness.
However, all outdoor activities involve a
degree of risk and the publishers accept
no responsibility for any injuries caused to
readers whilst following these walks. For
more advice on walking safely see page 144.
The mileage range shown on the front cover
is for guidance only – some walks may be
less than or exceed these distances.

Some of the walks may appear in other AA
books and publications.

Picture credits
The Automobile Association would like
to thank the following photographers,
companies and picture libraries for their
assistance in the preparation of this book.

Abbreviations for the picture credits are as
follows – (t) top; (b) bottom; (c) centre; (l)
left; (r) right; (AA) AA World Travel Library.

3 AA/A Newey; 7 Anthony Pilling/Alamy;
10 PrimrosePix/Alamy; 17 AA/A Newey;
21 Guy Edwardes Photography/Alamy; 44
David Martyn Hughes/Alamy; 62-63 James
Osmond/Alamy; 68 © Paul Glendell/Alamy;
86 Lee Pengelly/Alamy; 90 Derek Stone/
Alamy; 97 AA/G Edwardes; 107 Lee Pengelly/
Alamy; 114 Lee Pengelly/Alamy; 124 Andrew
Ray/Alamy; 140 James Osmond/Alamy.

Every effort has been made to trace the
copyright holders, and we apologise in
advance for any accidental errors. We would
be happy to apply the corrections in the
following edition of this publication.

Opposite: White chalk cliffs at Beer Head

40 Short Walks in

DEVON

Contents

Walk	Rating	Distance	Page

Rating

Each walk is rated for its relative difficulty compared to the other walks in this book. Walks marked +++ are likely to be shorter and easier with little total ascent. The hardest walks are marked +++

Walking in Safety

For advice and safety tips see page 144.

Introduction

There is no doubt that the most satisfying way to go exploring is on foot. The pace of life slows, you have the chance to absorb the landscape and your surroundings, and to stop to enjoy a particularly wonderful view. Devon has long attracted walkers looking for something of a challenge. The county is host to a good chunk of the South West Coast Path – the country's longest National Trail, measuring 630 miles (1,014m) from Minehead in Somerset to the shores of Poole Harbour in Dorset – and the rugged heights of Dartmoor, both justifiably renowned for their natural beauty. But Devon – England's third largest county – is also a place where less ambitious walkers can find a huge variety of short walks to enjoy.

Why Devon?

Devon is blessed with an extraordinary range of different landscapes. For a start, it is the only county in the country to have a north and a south coast. The north coast – including two thirds of the coastline of Exmoor National Park – is on the whole rugged and windswept, a mix of high cliffs and rocky coves, with long sandy beaches round the Taw–Torridge estuary. The south coast, on the other hand, is less wild: tranquil wooded river valleys and pretty riverside towns and villages, extremely popular with holidaymakers. And as you travel east along the south coast the character of the coastline changes again as you meet the World Heritage Jurassic Coast, where the cliffs tumble steeply into the sea.

Moving inland the walker is yet again faced with a choice. You can explore the raised granite plateau – the biggest area of granite in England at 368 square miles (953sq km) – that is Dartmoor National Park, lofty moorland studded with rocky tors, and steep-sided wooded river valleys. The Devon part of Exmoor National Park, a sandstone plateau altogether more forgiving than its more southerly neighbour, is known for its patchwork of small hedgebanked fields, remote farms and churches, and magnificent hog's-back cliffs towering above the Bristol Channel.

A Rural Landscape

Devon is an essentially rural county and the origins of rights of way date from the days when communication between remote settlements and farmsteads was on foot, and paths and green lanes developed as a means of getting from one place to another. One aspect of rural life in Devon that has changed over the last few years, however, has been the revitalisation of the village shop.

Opposite: Appledore from northam burrows

For many years pubs and shops struggled to survive in the remoter corners of the county, but now you will see community shops in small villages, where the local population has pulled together to either keep their shop open or, in some cases, start one from scratch. Relying largely on voluntary labour – and selling locally sourced food as well as that bought in from larger suppliers – such shops play a vital social role in the lives of rural villages. Rural pubs too are fighting their corner and tend to serve better food at more reasonable prices than those in the traditional holiday centres.

The 40 routes here are all intended to occupy a morning or afternoon, and every one is packed with interest, be it a visit to a historic fishing village, an exploration of a prehistoric settlement, or a stroll through a nature reserve. Enjoy every mile of it.

Using the Book

This collection of 40 walks is easy to use. Use the locator map, see opposite, to select your walk, then turn to the map and directions of your choice. The route of each walk is shown on a map and clear directions help you follow the walk. Each route is accompanied by background information about the walk and area.

INFORMATION PANELS

An information panel for each walk details the total distance, landscape, paths, parking, public toilets and any special conditions that apply, such as restricted access or level of dog friendliness. The minimum time suggested for the walk is for reasonably fit walkers and doesn't allow for stops.

ASCENT AND DIFFICULTY

An indication of the gradients you will encounter is shown by the rating ▲▲▲ (no steep slopes) to ▲▲▲ (several very steep slopes). Walks are also rated for difficulty. Walks marked ✚✚✚ are likely to be shorter and easier with little total ascent. The hardest walks are marked ✚✚✚.

MAPS AND START POINTS

There are 40 maps covering the walks. Some walks have a suggested option in the same area. Each walk has a suggested Ordnance Survey map. The start of each walk is given as a six-figure grid reference prefixed by two letters indicating which 100km square of the National Grid it refers to. You'll find more information on grid references on most Ordnance Survey maps.

CAR PARKING

Many of the car parks suggested are public, but occasionally you may find you have to park on the roadside or in a lay-by. Please be considerate when you leave your car, ensuring that access roads or gates are not blocked and that other vehicles can pass safely.

DOGS

We have tried to give dog owners useful advice about how dog friendly each walk is. Please respect other countryside users. Keep your dog under control, especially around livestock, and obey local bylaws and other dog control notices. Remember, it is against the law to let your dog foul in public areas, especially in villages and towns.

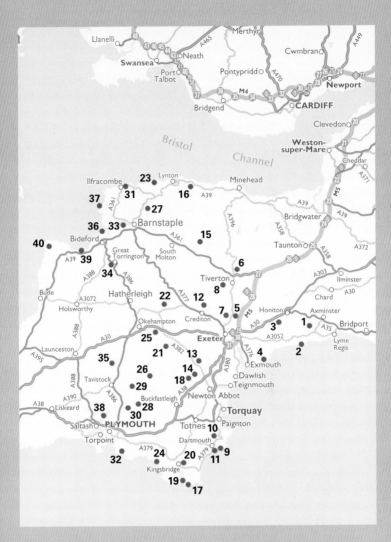

KEY TO WALKING MAPS

⇢	Walk Route		Built-up Area
❶	Route Waypoint		Woodland Area
– – –	Adjoining Path	🚻	Toilet
☀	Viewpoint	🅿	Car Park
•	Place of Interest	⊞	Picnic Area
⌂	Steep Section	)(	Bridge

THE RIVER COLY AND THE UMBORNE BROOK

The tranquil East Devon town of Colyton
has a chequered history.

In some ways the pretty East Devon town of Colyton is a rather misleading place. Situated in rolling countryside on the banks of the River Coly, the town has more than once won 'the prettiest village in Devonshire' accolade. The narrow, winding streets, attractive cottages, with hanging baskets and colourful gardens, give no clues as to why Colyton was once dubbed 'most rebellious town in Devon'. For this we must go back to the 1600s. The town supported Parliament in the Civil War in 1643, and was the scene of many skirmishes against Royalists based at Axminster. It also played a part in the Monmouth Rebellion of 1685, when more than 100 Colyton men – more than anywhere else in Devon – joined the Duke of Monmouth's army. Monmouth landed at Lyme Regis with 80 followers and managed to raise an army of 3,000, but was defeated by James II's army at Sedgemoor near Bridgwater in Somerset. In the trials that followed, the 'Bloody Assizes', 17 Colyton men were hanged, and 18 were transported to the West Indies. Only two of the latter made it back to Devon.

St Andrew's Church

The parish church is prominent in the view of Colyton towards the end of the walk. It also reflects the prosperous side of the town. There has been a church here since AD 700, but the current building is based on a Norman church from the mid-12th century. The most unusual feature is the rare octagonal lantern, set on the square Norman tower in the 15th century. The town's wool merchants are believed to have been inspired by similar towers in Flanders. There is a merchant's mark (representing a 'stapler' or wool merchant) on the floor slate marking the grave of Hugh Buckland in the chancel.

Iron Age Hill-fort

If you have time, it's worth going to have a look at Blackberry Camp Iron Age hill-fort, an English Heritage site signposted from the A3052 Colyton to Sidford road. Probably occupied by a community between the 1st and 2nd centuries AD, this D-shaped enclosure is a peaceful spot for a picnic.

Opposite: Sheep grazing Colyton

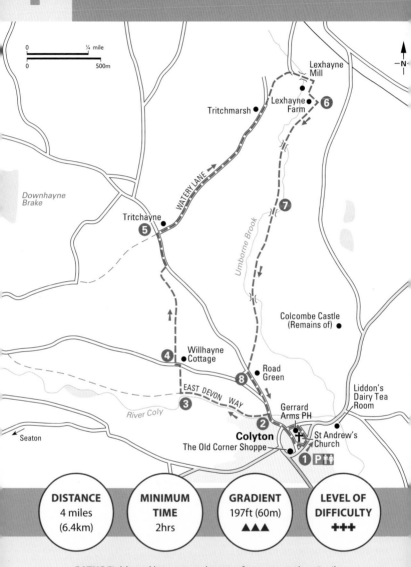

DISTANCE	MINIMUM TIME	GRADIENT	LEVEL OF DIFFICULTY
4 miles (6.4km)	2hrs	197ft (60m) ▲▲▲	+++

PATHS Fields and lanes, parts boggy after wet weather, 8 stiles
LANDSCAPE Level river meadows and rolling farmland
SUGGESTED MAP OS Explorer 116 Lyme Regis & Bridport
START/FINISH Grid reference: SY 246940
DOG FRIENDLINESS On lead through farmland
PARKING Paying car park in centre of Colyton (Dolphin Street)
PUBLIC TOILETS At car park

WALK 1 DIRECTIONS

❶ From the car park turn right past the toilets, then left into Lower Church Street. Turn left again at the Gerrard Arms into Rosemary Lane, then right into Vicarage Street opposite Colyton House. Go right, towards the river, and cross the bridge.

❷ Turn left through a kissing gate along the river bank on the East Devon Way (EDW). Follow the path through two kissing gates and continue to a footpath sign, before a kissing gate.

❸ Turn right up the left field edge, soon meeting the hedge on the left. Cross a stile on to the lane opposite Willhayne House and turn left.

❹ After a few paces turn right on a public bridleway. Pass The Stables and Willhayne Cottage and vineyard (producing white, rosé and little sparkling wine). Continue up a grassy hedged track to meet a lane. Turn left along the lane, rising gently.

❺ At Gate Cross turn right, signed 'Tritchayne', and walk down Watery Lane. Just after Tritchmarsh follow the footpath sign, right, on a wooden walkway. Go sharp left to a gate and left round the field. Ignore the next stile left; take the next small gate, bridge then gate and cross the paddock and the Umborne Brook via a gate and concrete walkway to Lexhayne Mill. The path runs between the house and yard to a kissing gate, then over the stile in the wire fence (the main line railway is ahead). Cross over the next stile, then head diagonally right for the drive to Lexhayne Farm. Cross a stile, and keep ahead through a hedge gap.

❻ Cross the field diagonally to the bottom corner, over a double gate and bridge and the big footbridge. Walk left, go over a stile, then keep ahead to cross the brook via a footbridge and double gate with the church ahead.

❼ Aim for the stile in the fence ahead right. Bear diagonally left to cross the brook via a double gate and bridge, then left. Cross a stile and two stiles and footbridges then diagonally cross the upper part of the next field. Walk downhill and cross a stile to the road.

❽ Turn left; pass the playground at Road Green, then cross the bridge. Take the first left (Vicarage Street) and go on to pass the church, through the town centre to Silver Street and the car park.

🍴 EATING AND DRINKING

The Gerrard Arms at the start of the walk is a free house with an attractive garden and bar food. Liddon's Dairy Tea Room, with inside and outside seating (and palms for sale) is passed on the way to Colyton Station, where there is a tea room on the platform. St Andrew's Garden, by the church, has picnic tables and covered seating.

HOOKEN CLIFFS AND BEER HEAD

An exploration above and below the chalk cliffs of East Devon's World Heritage Coast.

In late 2001, the 95-mile (155m) coast of East Devon and Dorset – from Exmouth to near Old Harry Rocks – was designated as England's first natural World Heritage Site on account of the unique insight it provides into 185 million years of the earth's history.

Beer is also famous for Honiton lace, a craft brought here by 16th-century Flemish refugees: the lace for Queen Victoria's wedding dress was made here at a cost of £1,000

The Jurassic Coast

Popularly known as 'the Jurassic Coast', this section of coast contains rocks from the Triassic, Jurassic and Cretaceous periods. Any walk on the South West Coast Path in this area will encounter a range of varied landscapes and wildlife habitats, from Budleigh Salterton's pebble beds and the towering red sandstone cliffs around Sidmouth to the fossil beds of Lyme Regis and Charmouth, and the extraordinary 17-mile (28km) shingle and pebble barrier known as Chesil Beach in Dorset. The village of Beer is surrounded by high cliffs of white chalk, formed over 70 million years ago during the Cretaceous period when this area was more like the present-day Gulf of Arabia in terms of climate.

The walk passes through the Hooken Undercliff (a 'slumped' section of chalk cliff), created in 1789, which today a magical place – a luxuriant tangle of trees and plants, a secret wilderness, and one of the most extraordinary spots on the whole 630-mile (1,014km) South West Coast Path.

A Smuggling Hotspot

The attractive seaside village of Beer is popular with families because of its lovely beach, but it also has a long history of smuggling.

The village's most infamous son was Jack Rattenbury, born in 1778, who took up a life of fishing and smuggling, with the occasional press-ganged stint in the Navy (and in gaol). It is said he used to store his contraband deep in the Beer Quarry caves, and in caves on the Hooken Undercliff.

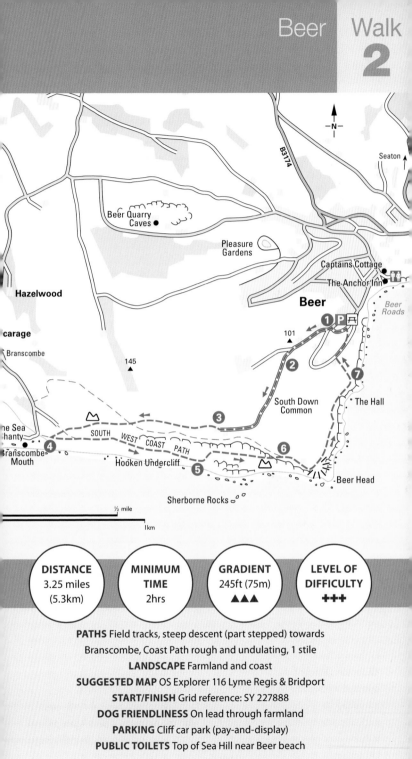

DISTANCE	MINIMUM TIME	GRADIENT	LEVEL OF DIFFICULTY
3.25 miles (5.3km)	2hrs	245ft (75m) ▲▲▲	+++

PATHS Field tracks, steep descent (part stepped) towards
Branscombe, Coast Path rough and undulating, 1 stile

LANDSCAPE Farmland and coast

SUGGESTED MAP OS Explorer 116 Lyme Regis & Bridport

START/FINISH Grid reference: SY 227888

DOG FRIENDLINESS On lead through farmland

PARKING Cliff car park (pay-and-display)

PUBLIC TOILETS Top of Sea Hill near Beer beach

WALK 2 DIRECTIONS

❶ From the car park turn left uphill past the entrance to Beer Head Caravan Park. Go through a bridlegate by a cattle grid, signed to Branscombe. The lane forks; take the left fork, soon passing through a bridlegate.

❷ Follow the track along the top edge of a field, with a wire fence right. Pass through a bridlegate by a cattle grid, and follow the track as it bears right towards an unusual two-storey building. Pass immediately to the right of the building and cottage, then bear slightly left and continue across South Down Common, with a wire fence right and views ahead to Sidmouth and High Peak (site of an Iron Age hill-fort).

❸ At the end of the field bear left through two gates into National Trust land at East Cliff. Keep straight on, soon reaching a very steep descent towards Branscombe beach. Pass a bridlepath (right) and a bench; bear slightly left downhill, between stands of gorse, to find very steeply descending steps that drop towards the coast, crossing a stile on route. Descend the left edge of the next field to pass through a gate in the corner on to the Coast Path.

❹ Turn left along the Coast Path through the Sea Shanty Caravan Park, a wonderful collection of wooden chalets scattered along the lower cliffs. At a rough fork keep straight on, noting high chalk cliffs ahead.

Follow the narrow path as it wends its way through the tangled jungle of the Hooken Undercliff, a secret and somewhat exotic wildlife paradise beneath friable chalk cliffs.

❺ Pass a small path leading to the beach; soon after your path bears inland a little and starts to ascend gently under willow and ash with tall chalk stacks now to the right. The path steepens and zig-zags left then right to reach a kissing gate onto the cliff top, at a path junction.

> **🍴 EATING AND DRINKING**
>
> There's a picnic area in the car park, or you can walk down Common Lane into Beer for a crab sandwich or fresh fish special at The Anchor Inn, which has a garden overlooking the beach. The lovely thatched Captains Cottage nearby offers traditional cream teas beautifully served on a glass cake stand. Fresh fish is on sale on the beach.

❻ Turn right along the Coast Path and on to Beer Head. Go through a kissing gate, and past the next one, after which the path bears left along the cliffs. Continue through a gateway, then a kissing gate. Follow the right edge of the next field and go through a bank, then bear left inland.

❼ Pass through a gate on to a hedged path, with the caravan park left, soon bearing right to the car park.

Opposite: White chalk cliffs at Beer Head

OTTERY ST MARY AND THE TUMBLING WEIR

There's more than meets the eye to this quiet East Devon town, situated in the lovely Otter Valley.

Scratch the surface of the attractive little East Devon town of Ottery St Mary and you'll be amazed: for literary connections and historic interest it's hard to beat. This is due to the fact that in the 18th century Ottery was a prosperous wool town, as evidenced by the large number of fine Georgian buildings, especially near the church. The Flexton, where the walk starts, was site of the town market and fair, granted by Royal Charter under Henry II in 1226.

Church of St Mary of Ottery

For a start there's the impressive Church of St Mary of Ottery: the original building here was extended between 1337 and 1342 as a collegiate church along similar lines (though less than half the size) to St Peter's Cathedral in Exeter. Many of the original buildings, such as the cloisters, chorister's house and choirboys' school have now gone; in 1545, at the Dissolution under Henry VIII, St Mary's became a rather grand parish church.

A Literary Heritage

Ottery is immensely proud of the fact that the poet and philosopher Samuel Taylor Coleridge was born here in 1772. Fascinating documents on display in the church record the handing over of the nine-year-old boy to Christ's Hospital on the death of his father, Revd John Coleridge (Master of the King's School), 'there to be educated and brought up among other poor children'. Both John and Samuel's mother Ann are buried in the church. Samuel was born in the School House near the church steps, which was demolished in 1884. A plaque on the wall records the event.

Woodbury Common

For an unexpected taste of 'wild country' in peaceful East Devon go for a walk on Woodbury Common, a large area of woodland and heath to the south-west of Ottery St Mary, criss-crossed by a network of paths and tracks. The highest point (600ft/183m) is crowned by Woodbury Castle, an Iron Age hill-fort.

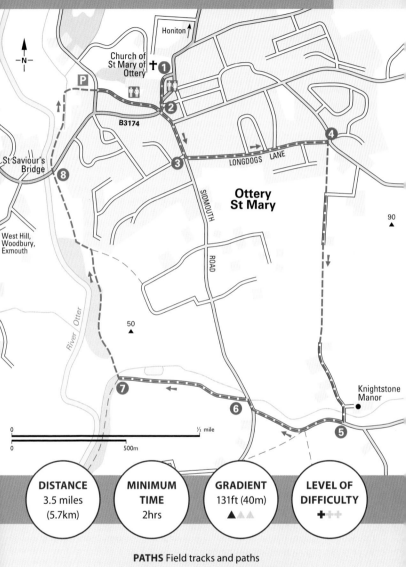

DISTANCE
3.5 miles
(5.7km)

MINIMUM TIME
2hrs

GRADIENT
131ft (40m)
▲▲▲

LEVEL OF DIFFICULTY
✚✚✚

PATHS Field tracks and paths
LANDSCAPE Farmland and town paths
SUGGESTED MAP OS Explorer 115 Exmouth & Sidmouth
START/FINISH Grid reference: SY 099956
DOG FRIENDLINESS On lead through farmland
PARKING Canaan Way car park (pay-and-display)
PUBLIC TOILETS The Flexton (near the church) and Hind Street

WALK 3 DIRECTIONS

1 From the church steps walk down Silver Street. Follow the lane to reach The Square, off which lanes run in several directions.

2 Cross the road; turn left past the TIC. Bear right up Tip Hill (Sidmouth Road), passing through a cutting at the top (there is a pavement on the left).

3 At the brow of the hill turn left along Longdogs Lane passing houses and eventually the primary school. The lane drops downhill to a crossroads.

4 Turn right on a signed bridleway between high hedges. Pass through two bridlegates; the path broadens to a track, passing through a bridlegate by Knightstone Cottages. Keep ahead as signed at a rounded fork. At the entrance to Orchard Cottage bear slightly right down a track to reach a drive at Knightstone Manor. Keep ahead, with a wall left, across a stream and through iron gates on to a lane.

> **🍴 EATING AND DRINKING**
>
> The Millstone Bakery in Mill Street – Ottery's only working bakery – produces all manner of delicious snacks to take away, including home-made pasties. You'll be assured of a friendly welcome (and soothing classical music) at Seasons Traditional Tearoom on Silver Street (closed Sunday and Monday), which has a small courtyard garden.

5 Turn right to a T-junction (Sidmouth Road). Cross with care and walk right for a few paces, then left through a kissing gate on a footpath. Follow the track along the lower right edge of a field. Eventually pass through a metal gate and drop to a footpath junction.

6 Keep on through a gateway (yellow arrow). Follow the right field-edge and go through a gate into woodland; the River Otter can be seen left. Follow the narrow path, later climbing steps into a field via a small gate; turn left.

7 At the next gate turn left; descend overgrown steps along the left edge of a rough field, towards a gate/footbridge. Cross over; follow a narrow path through Indian balsam and willow eventually on to an embankment. Turn right along the bank, which curves left to a kissing gate on to the B3174 opposite the derelict mill.

8 Cross with care and turn left. Just before St Saviour's Bridge turn right on a tarmac footpath along the river bank to the drive to the Tumbling Weir Hotel. Cross over to pass the tumbling weir and information panel; follow the tarmac path along the leat. Turn right on the first bridge; keep ahead, bearing left past the playground and right at the next junction to meet Canaan Way opposite Hind Street. Cross over; where Hind Street bears right towards The Square turn left along Saddlers Lane. Turn left for the church.

Opposite: Parish church of Ottery St Mary

THE OTTER ESTUARY NATURE RESERVE

Along the banks of the peaceful River Otter
to the pebble ridge at Budleigh Salterton.

Peaceful, tranquil, lush, idyllic – words that could easily be applied to this stroll along the banks of the River Otter. The river wends its way to meet the sea just east of Budleigh Salterton, its lower reaches a haven for a wealth of birdlife. The combination of the serene river meadows and level paths – and the chance for an ice cream in Budleigh Salterton, or tea at Otterton Mill – makes this an ideal family walk.

The Otter Estuary Nature Reserve

The nature reserve, south of White Bridge, is a Site of Special Scientific Interest (SSSI) and nationally important wildlife habitat, one of the smallest in the south-west. The estuary was much more extensive in the past, and 500 years ago cargo ships could travel up river as far as Otterton. Today it provides a haven for all kinds of birdlife, best seen between October and March. Oystercatchers, dunlins and other wading birds come to feed here. The high numbers of wigeon and teal attract peregrine falcons, sparrowhawks and mink. Three-quarters of the estuary has been colonised by saltmarsh, which is also home to warblers in the summer months, linnets and greenfinches all year round, and kingfishers in winter. To catch the action, stop for a while in the bird hide passed on Point ❷ and watch the activity on the waters below .

Along the route of the walk, look out for the smallest of the grebe family; the little grebe, although rare in Devon, has been spotted near White Bridge. Naturally clumsy on land, all members of the grebe family become experts when they hit the water. The little grebe (about 10–12in/25–30cm long), often called the 'dabchick', is a busy little bird, diving and bobbing up again in its search for food. Interestingly, after many years in decline, otter numbers in Devon have steadily increased since the early 1980s, and they have now been recorded on every Devon river.

Man has influenced the shape of the estuary for thousands of years. Evidence of a Roman villa has been unearthed at South Farm on Otterton Point, and it is thought that the Romans – or maybe even Iron Age peoples – collected salt from the marshes.

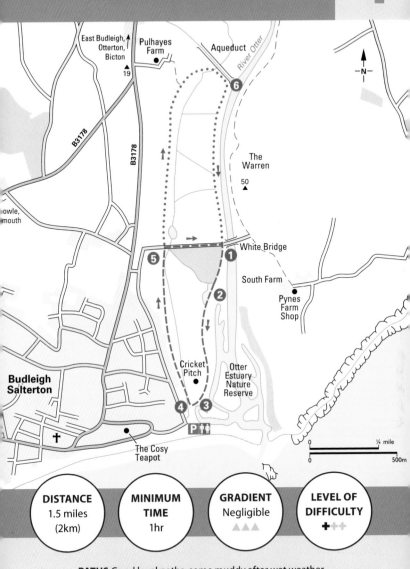

DISTANCE	MINIMUM TIME	GRADIENT	LEVEL OF DIFFICULTY
1.5 miles (2km)	1hr	Negligible ▲▲▲	✦✦✦

PATHS Good level paths, some muddy after wet weather

LANDSCAPE Riverside meadows and saltmarsh

SUGGESTED MAP OS Explorer 115 Exeter & Sidmouth

START/FINISH Grid reference: SY 074830

DOG FRIENDLINESS Keep on lead through nature reserve

PARKING Laneside parking near White Bridge

PUBLIC TOILETS In Limekiln car park, Budleigh Salterton

WALK 4 DIRECTIONS

❶ The walk starts on the west side of White Bridge. Pass through a small gate, following Coast Path signs to Budleigh Salterton along the right bank of the river. This popular part of the path is very level and well surfaced. The large pebble bar at the mouth of the estuary can be seen ahead, created by a huge storm: plans to blast a shipping channel through this were dropped with the coming of the railway in 1897.

❷ The Coast Path runs along an embankment, built by Napoleonic prisoners of war as part of a scheme to drain the land to form the meadows seen today. Pass a bird hide overlooking the Otter, in which there is information about identifying birds seen on the water and in the saltmarsh. Soon after, the path bears right past the cricket pitch to meet a footpath post, with the Coast Path signed ahead.

❸ Turn right on a footpath to pass the children's playground. Go through a kissing gate and keep straight on as signed. Bear right across the drive to Budleigh Salterton cricket club to another footpath sign.

❹ Keep ahead up a hedged path, signed to White Bridge. Cross a grassy area with a house left, and keep ahead on a path that runs up the western edge of the floodplain: this half of the walk will be much quieter in terms of numbers of people. Note a sandstone cliff left, topped with huge oak trees, which would have marked the edge of the estuary before it silted up in the 15th century. Eventually pass through a kissing gate, then another; a third leads on to the lane.

> ### 🍴 EATING AND DRINKING
> Follow the Coast Path in to Budleigh for excellent locally made ice cream and the delightful Cosy Teapot for a cream tea. Pynes Farm Shop near the start of the walk sells snacks, Salcombe Dairy ice cream and takeaway drinks. The Otterton Mill Restaurant is open daily from 10am to 5pm and serves a great range of delicious home-made dishes, and has a Devon Food Shop and bakery.

❺ Turn right for 0.25 miles (400m) to find White Bridge. Note that the walk can be extended for a further 1.5 miles (2.4km) from this point. For the longer walk cross the lane and go through the kissing gate, and follow the signed path ahead, which eventually leads into a track (note that this is used by cattle and can be very muddy). Where the track bears left towards Pulhayes Farm, bear right over a stile; keep ahead to cross another on to a track, and turn right. The embanked track curves towards the river.

❻ On meeting the River Otter turn right through a gate (for Otterton Mill turn left here for 1 mile/1.6km) and follow the river back to White Bridge.

THE NATIONAL TRUST AT KILLERTON

A gentle parkland and woodland walk around
the National Trust's beautiful Killerton Estate.

This gentle exploration around the National Trust estate at Killerton, given
to the Trust by Sir Richard Acland in 1944, uses a variety of well-maintained
public footpaths and bridleways, but does not give access to the gardens. To
visit them you must pay an entrance fee (NT members free).

Killerton is well worth a visit: quite apart from the house, rebuilt in 1778–79
to the design of John Johnson, and delightful gardens (with colour-coded
waymarked walks) there is a National Trust shop, tea room and plant centre
in the old stable block and courtyard, as well as a playground and picnic
area. The whole estate covers 6,400 acres (2,592ha) and includes Ashclyst
Forest, 2 miles (3.2km) to the east (with waymarked walks), the Red Lion pub
in Broadclyst, to the south, and the disused paper mill by Ellerhayes Bridge.
You can see the gatehouse and old chapel of the Acland's original house at
Columbjohn on the optional extension to the walk.

A Glorious Setting

The park and gardens at Killerton were created in the late 18th century,
making full use of the contours of the natural landscape, and are
characterised by a wide variety of exotic tree species, including tall
Wellingtonias (named after the Duke of Wellington). As you enter the
parkland at Point ❷ you pass some splendid examples of cedar of Lebanon
and holm oak, and a beautiful weeping willow on an island in a pond (on
the left). Just past the house the walk leads uphill near the memorial to Sir
Thomas Dyke Acland, and you can enjoy good views west towards the Exe
Valley and beyond to Cosdon Hill on Dartmoor.

Columbjohn Chapel

If you decide to visit Columbjohn Chapel you will see that the burial ground is
dominated by the graves of the Acland family, as well as the tombstone of the
Silverton stationmaster. Unfortunately the chapel is used as a storeroom and
kept locked, but the stone doorway and simple bell tower are quite charming.
It's an ideal spot to pause for a while and enjoy a quiet moment of reflection.

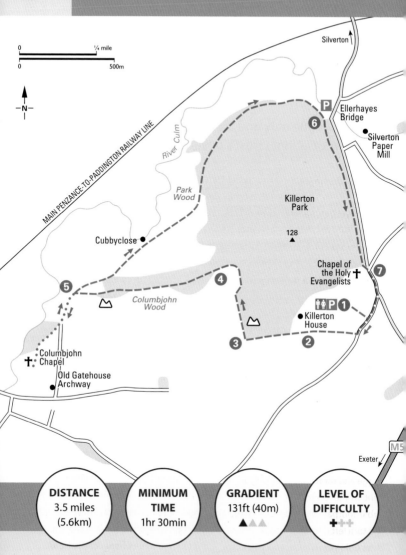

DISTANCE	MINIMUM TIME	GRADIENT	LEVEL OF DIFFICULTY
3.5 miles (5.6km)	1hr 30min	131ft (40m) ▲▲▲	+++

PATHS Good footpaths, bridleways and farm tracks, some muddy

LANDSCAPE Gently undulating woodland and parkland

SUGGESTED MAP OS Explorer 114 Exeter & the Exe Valley

START/FINISH Grid reference: SS 977002

DOG FRIENDLINESS Keep on lead in park

PARKING National Trust car park plus overflow car park

PUBLIC TOILETS Between car park and stable courtyard

WALK 5 DIRECTIONS

❶ From the car park return to the road and turn right to reach the gate and cattle grid at the entrance drive to Killerton House. Follow the public footpath sign towards the house, with a fence right, passing the stables and courtyard from where ticket holders approach the house.

❷ On reaching the wall in front of the house bear left, and continue with the wall left to pass formal gardens. Shortly after pass through a kissing gate in the hedge ahead into a large sloping field.

🍴 EATING AND DRINKING

Killerton House has the Garden Tea Room (when the house is open) and Orchard Tea Room, and there is a good pub – the Red Lion – attractively situated by the church in Broadclyst, 2.5 miles (4km) south on the B3181.

---

❸ Turn right uphill, keeping by the hedge and then iron fence on your right. At the top of the field ignore the public footpath sign 'Bluebell Gate', and turn left down across the field to enter Columbjohn Wood (look out for mountain bikers) through a small gate.

❹ Turn left, and immediately branch left again on the higher path round a wooden barrier, which leads gradually downhill. Leave the wood by another kissing gate, and keep straight on to meet and follow a farm track. For the optional route to visit 16th-century Columbjohn Chapel, keep ahead; after 250yds/229m cross the stile on the right to enter a field. Keeping the wood on your right, pass a cottage to arrive at the chapel. Cross another stile to gain the grassy drive to the chapel; look left to see the old gatehouse. Retrace your steps through the field back to Point ❺.

❺ On the main route turn right and follow this delightful level track through woods and fields around the edge of the estate, ignoring any paths leading right (into the gardens). The River Culm can be seen on your left, but you will be more aware of the main Penzance-to-Paddington railway. The track reaches the road by Ellerhayes Bridge.

❻ Do not go on to the road; turn right to follow the edge of the undulating parkland and woods, keeping the road on your left. You will pass through several gates on an NT bridlepath, which eventually goes through two gates and bears right to join a gravel track. Turn left downhill to pass the entrance to the Chapel of the Holy Evangelists, built in the Norman style in 1842 for the Aclands, their tenants and employees, to replace the one at Columbjohn.

❼ Meet the road. Keep ahead downhill, then right at the junction, and right again into the car park.

KNIGHTSHAYES COURT

An easy amble through the woods and parkland of one of the country's finest Victorian country houses.

A wander around the scenic rolling expanse of 200-acre (81ha) Knightshayes Estate near Bolham is to take a step back in time to the days when wealthy Victorians commissioned the construction of grand country houses in idyllic surroundings. The estate has been under the ownership of the National Trust since 1973, and somehow manages to swallow up the huge number of visitors each year – however busy the house and gardens may be, you will soon have the park virtually to yourself on this walk.

A Grand Country House

Knightshayes Court was built for the lace millionaire Sir John Heathcoat-Amory, and designed by the eccentric architect William Burges. It's an imposing and rather romantic building, sited to give views over the family factory on the banks of the River Exe in the valley below.

The building was commissioned in 1867, and the foundation stone laid two years later; work was completed in 1874, by which time Burges had fallen out with his employer and been replaced by J D Crace. The beautiful gardens were designed by Edward Kemp, and include a wonderful topiary of a fox and hounds, as well as many specimen trees, rare shrubs, amazing seasonal colours and a huge walled kitchen garden, that has recently been restored to full working order.

Knightshayes also has a rare stické court – there are only two known in the UK – dating from 1907: stické is a racket-and-ball, court-based game invented by the military in the late 19th century.

Springtime Garden

In springtime Knightshayes' woodland garden is carpeted with delicate flowers: wood anemones, wood sorrel, lesser celandine, pink purslane and bluebells. In late autumn look out for fungi – Britain has 12,000 species – often found on dead wood or the base of tree trunks. You may spot the oak milk cep (reputed to smell like bed bugs!) or the penny bun, a curiously shaped boletus.

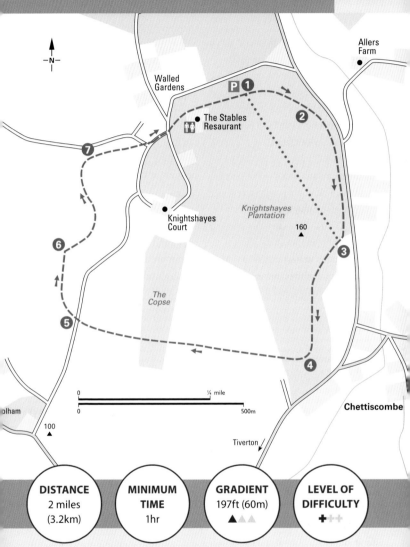

DISTANCE	MINIMUM TIME	GRADIENT	LEVEL OF DIFFICULTY
2 miles (3.2km)	1hr	197ft (60m) ▲▲▲	+++

PATHS Woodland paths (some muddy after wet weather) and pathless grassland

LANDSCAPE Woodland and parkland

SUGGESTED MAP OS Explorer 114 Exeter & the Exe Valley

START/FINISH Grid reference: SS 962153

DOG FRIENDLINESS On lead in parkland, can run free in woods

PARKING Knightshayes Court car park (free) **PUBLIC TOILETS** At The Stables, Knightshayes Court **NOTE** The park is open all year round

WALK 6 DIRECTIONS

❶ The walk starts at the sign for the Impey Walk, opposite the disabled parking area just below the public parking area behind The Stables. Follow the broad woodland path into Knightshayes Plantation.

❷ The path soon drops to run parallel to a lane. Follow it through mixed woodland to a path junction.

❸ To shorten the walk to 1.5 miles (2.4km) turn sharp right to return to the car park. For the parkland stretch on the main route keep ahead as signed, descending gently through beech woodland.

❹ At the next footpath sign turn right through an iron gate into The Blackeries. Follow park railings, with a wire fence right. Pass through iron gates into and out of The Copse, and into parkland. Keep straight ahead; look right for a wonderful view of the front of the house. Head towards the park railings, aiming for a big gate a few paces right of a smaller one.

❺ Cross the main drive and go through a gate to reach a waymark post; follow

> ### 🍴 EATING AND DRINKING
> As well as delicious cakes and biscuits you can sample produce from the kitchen garden in The Stables Restaurant at Knighthayes – not only fresh, but also in the form of jams, chutneys and pickles to take away. Local wines are also on sale, and even home-made dog treats.

the arrow to pass beneath huge horse chestnut and oak trees across rough grassland. As the land drops steeply, with a wooden seat left, bear right downhill past a fenced plantation left, heading for a five-bar gate (slippery after wet weather). Pass through, soon bearing left across a small stream.

❻ Keep briefly ahead, to the left of a fenced-off pond among trees, to find a wooden post on the left; turn right and head uphill, parallel to the stream.

❼ Pass through a gate in railings at the top, then keep left of Azalea Dell (and pond). Turn left to find a waymark post above left, then turn right on a tarmac path to meet the drive. Turn left towards The Stables and car park, passing the Victorian walled garden.

> ### 🌿 IN THE AREA
> For further insight into the social history of this area visit Coldharbour Mill at Uffculme (just off the M5 east of Tiverton), a 200-year-old woollen and worsted mill, built by Thomas Fox in 1799. The mill closed in 1981, but the original machinery is still in place; the textile museum opened in 1982, with guided tours and 'steam up' days. Refreshments are available in the Gill Box Restaurant.

THE MEANDERING EXE AT BRAMPFORD SPEKE

Water-meadows, ox-bow lakes and herons – a post-Sunday lunch amble along the river bank of the Exe.

There is a secluded piece of Devonshire countryside lying just north of Exeter. Few would think of turning off the A377 Exeter to Crediton road to have a look around – but here is a beautiful area of undulating woods and farmland in the Exe Valley. Brampford Speke is just one of the pleasant cob and thatch villages that lies tucked away here, situated on a low cliff of red sandstone overhanging the River Exe as it meanders lazily through its flood plain. You almost feel as if the river is relieved to reach Brampford Speke and is taking a rest after a long journey from its source. This is high on Exmoor to the north, from where it tumbles down through deeply wooded combes, past the castle at Tiverton, under the bridge at Bickleigh and on to the flood plain.

Ox-bow Lakes and Tucking Mills

As you stroll along the banks of the Exe you may notice a number of places where it appears that the river has changed – or is going to change – its course. This is a common flood plain feature. The erosive power of the water alters as the river swings through the level plain, and starts to cut deeply into the outer bends of its course. At the same time silt and alluvial debris carried in its waters are deposited on the inner bends where the current is less strong. As time goes on the process intensifies until eventually the river cuts across the bend and carves a new course, leaving behind a curved 'ox-bow' lake, separate from the river.

The fertile red soils of the Exe Valley, derived from Permian sandstones, provide good arable farmland and meadows, the best agricultural land in Devon. The area has been thickly populated and farmed for centuries. At Upton Pyne a group of Bronze Age burial barrows has been dated to around 2000 BC. It was recorded in the Domesday Book (1086) that of 99 mills in Devon, three-quarters were located in or east of the Exe Valley. This was an important cloth-making area in the 14th century, with a large number of fulling ('tucking') mills (where woven cloth was flattened to improve its appearance). A tax return of 1332 recorded that 38 'tuckers' were sufficiently well off to pay tax, and that a large percentage came from this area.

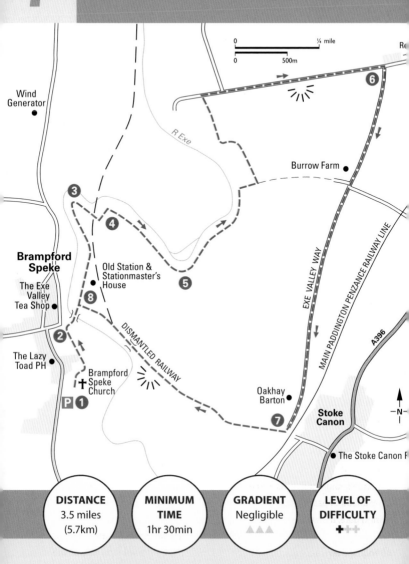

DISTANCE	MINIMUM TIME	GRADIENT	LEVEL OF DIFFICULTY
3.5 miles (5.7km)	1hr 30min	Negligible ▲▲▲	✚✚✚

PATHS Grassy field paths, tracks and country lanes, 2 stiles

LANDSCAPE Water-meadows and farmland

SUGGESTED MAP OS Explorer 114 Exeter & the Exe Valley

START/FINISH Grid reference: SX 927982

DOG FRIENDLINESS Livestock in some fields

PARKING On laneside near St Peter's Church, Brampford Speke

PUBLIC TOILETS None on route

WALK 7 DIRECTIONS

❶ Follow the Exe Valley Way (EVW) footpath signs down the lane to the right of the church, then left through the churchyard. Leave via a gate, and follow the path through a kissing gate. The path brings you onto a lane at a wooden kissing gate under a lychgate.

❷ Turn right and follow the footpath signs downhill to cross the River Exe over a large wooden bridge. Bear left across the meadow, following footpath signs. Ignore the footpath sign pointing right and go through a gateway in the hedge ahead; keep close to the river (on your left).

❸ Follow the river as it loops around the flood plain. Cross the old railway line via two kissing gates. On the left you'll see old railway bridge piers in the river and look out for grey herons.

❹ Immediately through the second gate drop down left to the river and continue straight on. Cross a stile and keep ahead to pass through a double kissing gate, then later cross a stile.

❺ Follow the river; after a mile (1.6km) the path bears right away from the river down a track to a kissing gate. Turn immediately left along another track. At the next footpath post go straight on (ignoring EVW signs left) along a green lane. The hedges disappear and the lane crosses farmland, ending at a road on the edge of Rewe.

ⓘ EATING AND DRINKING

Check out the cosy Exe Valley Tea Shop (and village stores) in Chapel Road, which serves teas, coffee and light lunches (evening meals some days; closed Tuesdays and Thursdays), with a covered outside seating area, which is ideal for dog walkers and families. The village pub The Lazy Toad (free house) is also an exellent option for a pint and a meal.

❻ Turn right along the lane towards Stoke Canon to pass the old cross at Burrow Farm. Carry straight on to pass Oakhay Barton. Note the Stoke Canon level crossing on the Exeter–Tiverton line ahead.

❼ Just before the level crossing follow the footpath sign right through a kissing gate and along a fenced path. Pass through another kissing gate and metal gate to join a dismantled railway line. Pass through another kissing gate and go straight on. A kissing gate leads over a small bridge and into a copse. Another kissing gate leads back into the meadows (marshy in winter, but there is a small wooden footbridge, right, for use at such times) and to the footbridge over the Exe.

❽ Once you're over the bridge, retrace your steps up the path, turning left at the lychgate and then back through the churchyard to your car.

THE BUZZARDS WALK

A walk through peaceful hillside woods
and river banks in mid-Devon.

There are three, little-known but wonderful, areas of National Trust woodland – Cross's Wood, Thongsleigh Wood and Huntland Wood – tucked away in the secluded, undulating mid-Devon countryside to the west of Tiverton. This walk, very much off the beaten track, explores these lovely woodlands that are full of interest all year round. They seem to literally drape over the steep hillsides above the valley of the tiny River Dart, which runs into the River Exe at nearby Bickleigh.

There are several excellent picnic spots along the route, the best one being reached at Point ❹ where you can take a break on a high level open area after climbing up through Cross's Wood. It also gives you the opportunity to spend some quality time admiring that magnificent bird of prey so typical of this kind of landscape – the buzzard.

Buzzards

Watching a pair of common buzzards gliding through the sky has to be one of the most magnificent sights above the hills and valleys of the West Country. Using updraughts to soar overhead, their broad wings held forward and wing feathers extended, these most common of the larger raptors scan the ground below for their prey – small mammals, and rabbits in particular. Their characteristic 'whee-eur' call is frequently heard in hilly country, and if you're lucky enough to see one perched upright on a fence post you will notice it has a heavily barred tail, a small head and a black, hooked bill. With the decline in persecution by gamekeepers, and with a plentiful supply of rabbits, the buzzard population now runs to tens of thousands.

By contrast the scarce honey buzzard is one of the country's rarest breeders. It lives on a diet of wild bees and their honey, as well as on other insects. This rather refined food source may be supplemented occasionally by small mammals. The honey buzzard is only a summer visitor to southern England, and fewer than a dozen pairs attempt to nest each year. They are very unusual in this part of Devon but have been spotted over the Haldon Hills to the south-west of Exeter.

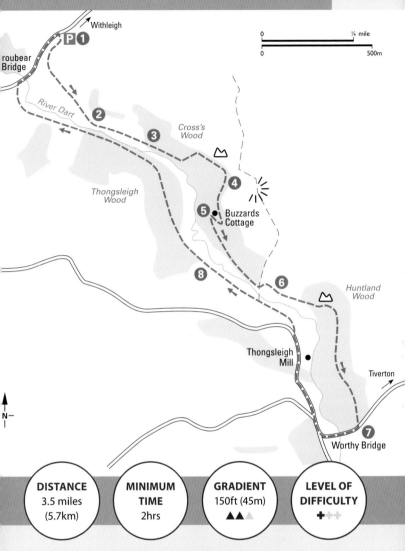

roubear
Bridge

River Dart

Cross's
Wood

Thongsleigh
Wood

Buzzards
Cottage

Huntland
Wood

Thongsleigh
Mill

Tiverton

N

Worthy Bridge

DISTANCE	MINIMUM TIME	GRADIENT	LEVEL OF DIFFICULTY
3.5 miles (5.7km)	2hrs	150ft (45m) ▲▲▲	✛✛✛

PATHS Waymarked paths, tracks (some muddy) and quiet lanes, 2 stiles
LANDSCAPE Wooded hillsides and river banks
SUGGESTED MAP OS Explorer 114 Exeter & the Exe Valley
START/FINISH Grid reference: SS 905121
DOG FRIENDLINESS Dogs should be kept under control, livestock in some fields
PARKING A narrow lane (No Through Road) leads to NT Buzzards car park from
B3137 near sign to parish church **PUBLIC TOILETS** None on route

WALK 8 DIRECTIONS

1 From the car park cross the stile into a field, and turn right. At the hedge ahead bear left and walk to the wood. Descend steeply at the wood edge, heading for a gate and a water trough.

2 Once through the gate go straight ahead, keeping the hedge left. Go through a gate and continue with the tiny River Dart on the right. Before the bridge turn left at the waymarker, through a small gate into another field. Turn right, keeping the high hedge right.

3 Leave the field through the next gate, which leads on to a broad track which rises through Cross's Wood. Soon after passing a bench a waymarker directs you left, off the track and back into the woods up a fairly steep path, which can be muddy in places. Continue to climb until the path reaches a wide track at the top of the woods.

4 Turn right to follow the track gently downhill, through a gate into an open area where it zig-zags more steeply downhill.

5 Pass Buzzards Cottage and follow the track left to join the riverside track. Follow the track ahead; before the bridge over the river (right), turn left on a broad track. After a few paces turn right over a stile and plank bridge to enter a field.

6 Keep the high hedge left and walk through the field to reach a gate into Huntland Wood. Follow the path uphill. Eventually it joins a track; bear right. The track levels off and leads through the upper wood before descending to leave the wood at a lane.

7 Turn right downhill, cross the Dart at Worthy Bridge, turn right at the next junction (signed 'Cruwys Morchard'), eventually passing Thongsleigh Mill (right). Where the lane bends left, go straight ahead through a gate on to a track. Where this drops to the river keep ahead, eventually passing through a gate and into Thongsleigh Wood.

8 Continue along the track, with the river, right. At a gate leave the wood and enter meadows; the path here is faint but continues straight ahead. The next metal gate leads on to a lane. Turn right over Groubear Bridge and climb back up the lane to the car park.

> ### 🍴 EATING AND DRINKING
>
> There is nothing very close by, but there is a pub at Pennymoor, 5 miles (8km) further west. The Cruwys Arms is not open at lunchtime Monday to Friday. The Mountpleasant Inn at Nomansland is open all day and serves good food. There's also the Cadeleigh Arms at Cadeleigh to the south of the walk, with real ale, good food and a pretty garden, but it's a bit of a trek to get there.

WARTIME SECRETS AT INNER FROWARD POINT

The delights of Coleton Fishacre –
and a surprise on the cliffs near Kingswear.

This is a walk that's full of surprises. It starts through fields above the sheltered valley containing the lovely National Trust house and gardens at Coleton Fishacre, then runs along a particularly beautiful piece of the South West Coast Path (much of which was purchased by the National Trust in 1982) with wonderful views towards the Mew Stone off the coast. Shetland ponies have been allowed to graze freely here in the past to encourage regeneration of the indigenous vegetation. Further on along the path you will find all sorts of strange concrete structures scattered about the cliffs, causing you to wonder what on earth it is you've stumbled across. The scenery changes again as you approach the eastern side of the Dart estuary, with fine views of the 15th-century Dartmouth Castle (its opposite number, Kingswear Castle, is just out sight). For sheer variety and constantly changing themes, this walk is very hard to beat.

An Arts and Crafts House

Given to the National Trust in 1982 by Roland Smith, Coleton Fishacre enjoys a spectacular setting in this very quiet corner of South Devon – it's very much off the beaten track. The house, reflecting the Arts and Crafts tradition, was designed and built in 1925–26 for Rupert and Lady Dorothy D'Oyly Carte, of Gilbert and Sullivan fame. It is sited at the head of a deep, sheltered combe, providing the perfect environment for its 15-acre (6ha) sub-tropical garden, based around a succession of streams and water features that fall gently down the narrow combe towards the sea at Pudcombe Cove.

The remains of Kingswear Castle (built 1491–1502) sit on the east side of the Dart estuary. Similar in shape to the square tower at Dartmouth Castle on the opposite shore, it was abandoned soon after 1643, outclassed by the range of guns available at its counterpart (see Walk 11), and today belongs to the Landmark Trust and is available as holiday accommodation. The official title of the group of buildings encountered on the coast path south of Kingswear is the Inner Froward Point Coast Defence Battery, dating from the Second World War and almost complete, apart from the guns.

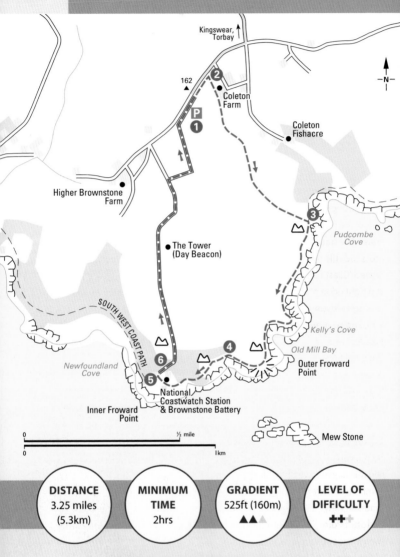

Kingswear, Torbay

162

Coleton Farm

Coleton Fishacre

Higher Brownstone Farm

The Tower (Day Beacon)

Pudcombe Cove

SOUTH WEST COAST PATH

Kelly's Cove

Old Mill Bay

Newfoundland Cove

Outer Froward Point

National Coastwatch Station & Brownstone Battery

Inner Froward Point

Mew Stone

0 ½ mile
0 1km

DISTANCE	MINIMUM TIME	GRADIENT	LEVEL OF DIFFICULTY
3.25 miles (5.3km)	2hrs	525ft (160m) ▲▲▲	✛✛✛

PATHS Undulating coast path, tracks, 2 stiles
LANDSCAPE Farmland and coast
SUGGESTED MAP OS Explorer OL20 South Devon
START/FINISH Grid reference: SX 905510
DOG FRIENDLINESS Dogs should be kept under control at all times
PARKING Higher Brownstone NT car park (free)
PUBLIC TOILETS None on route

WALK 9 DIRECTIONS

❶ From the car park entrance turn right along the lane. At a sign 'link to Coast Path' turn right through a kissing gate to pass to the right of a cream-coloured house. The fenced path hugs the left edge of a field before dropping to meet a track.

❷ Bear right (rejoining the permitted path through Coleton Farm) and follow the hedged track towards the coast. The track leads to two gates: cross the stile to the left of the left one, signed 'Coast Path'. Keep along the top right edge of the field. Pass through a kissing gate at the field end, and continue along the hedge. Pass a gate in the hedge and continue downhill through small stands of gorse to cross a stile on to Coleton Cliffs. Bear left steeply downhill to meet the Coast Path.

❸ Turn right. The path drops steeply, then levels off before climbing above Old Mill Bay followed by a steep climb up to Outer Froward Point, with fantastic views towards Slapton Sands and Start Point. The path undulates, then climbs steeply to reach the back of Froward Cove. Follow signs 'Coast Path' left for Kingswear.

❹ Pass through a gate, then 200yds (183m) later follow coast path signs left (keep ahead if you wish to shorten the walk and miss the Second World War remains, turning right on meeting the track that returns to the car park). Continue very steeply downhill through a wooded section. The path zig-zags down to Inner Froward Point, eventually following a metal railing.

❺ The lookout (once housing a searchlight) is the next landmark. Look towards the mouth of the Dart River to see Dartmouth Castle, then follow 104 uneven steps up the cliff to reach a gun emplacement. Ascend the miniature railway line and keep to the concrete walkway and steps to pass through some disused wartime buildings. At the top there is a junction of paths and a wooden footpath sign.

❻ Keep straight ahead, signed 'Higher Brownstone car park', up a lane (tarmacked in places) that climbs quite steeply. Just before passing through a gate note a 'link to Coast Path' sign right (see Point ❹). The lane levels to pass the 80ft (24m) day beacon, where locals also used to light fires to aid fishermen at sea at night. Follow the lane back to the car park.

🍴 **EATING AND DRINKING**

The nearest food and drink – apart from the National Trust café and restaurant at Coleton Fishacre when open – is in Kingswear where you will find The Royal Dart by the ferry slipway; The Ship Inn by the church; and The Steam Packet on the road to the lower ferry.

GREENWAY AND THE RIVER DART

A lovely walk through the woods and fields of Agatha Christie's Greenway Estate in the beautiful Dart Valley.

The wooded valley of the River Dart has been a holiday hot spot for the rich and famous for centuries, and in 1938 the crime novelist Agatha Christie bought the lovely house and gardens at Greenway, and used it as a summer home until her death in 1976. Although she never wrote any books there, her work is closely linked to south Devon, in particular the art deco Burgh Island Hotel (see Walk 24). The National Trust acquired the property and 300 acres (122ha) of land in 2000, and the gardens and house (set in the 1950s) are open to the public. Parking is very limited (and has to be pre-booked), and visitors are encouraged to arrive by greener methods – foot, bicycle or ferry.

Activity on the Dart

There has been a crossing point at what is now Greenway Quay since at least the Bronze and Iron Ages. Pretty Dittisham, on the other bank, witnessed some activity in the Second World War when in June 1944 the Dart provided safe anchorage for invasion landing craft gathering in preparation for D-Day: the building today housing the Anchor Stone Café was a first-aid post at that time. The passenger ferry to Dittisham can be summoned by ringing a bell.

The Dart is no stranger to all manner of craft. Legend has it Phoenician galleys and later Viking longboats ventured up it, and in the Middle Ages cog boats brought wine from the continent to Totnes. In keeping with this maritime heritage Greenway, then a Tudor mansion (and later remodelled in Georgian style) was the birthplace of Sir Humphrey Gilbert in 1539, a favourite of Queen Elizabeth I, who founded the colony of Newfoundland while trying to find the North West Passage.

While You're There

Take a ride on the Paignton & Dartmouth Steam Railway – you will no doubt hear the whistle on this walk – there's a station nearby at Churston. The line starts at Paignton, runs past Goodrington Sands to Churston, then through Greenway Tunnel on route to Kingswear. You can link your trip with a cruise along the Dart to Totnes, then take a bus back to Paignton.

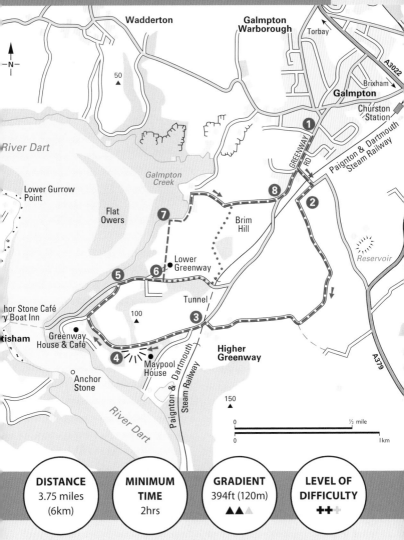

Galmpton

DISTANCE	MINIMUM TIME	GRADIENT	LEVEL OF DIFFICULTY
3.75 miles (6km)	2hrs	394ft (120m) ▲▲▲	✚✚✚

PATHS Paths and tracks, rolling parkland, one tidal section (optional), 3 stiles

LANDSCAPE Rolling farmland, river valley **SUGGESTED MAP** OS Explorer OL20 South Devon **START/FINISH** Grid reference: SX 888561

DOG FRIENDLINESS On lead through farmland and Greenway Estate

PARKING Laneside in village centre near primary school

PUBLIC TOILETS None on route **NOTE** The proposed route runs along a short section of foreshore; at times of high spring tides the alternative route (marginally shorter) will avoid the possibility of wet feet

WALK 10 DIRECTIONS

1 Start from the junction of Old Road and Greenway Road, by Galmpton primary school. Follow Greenway Road uphill out of the village, soon turning left on Kennel Lane over the Paignton & Dartmouth Steam Railway.

2 Turn right on a bridlepath (Combe Lane) that soon bears left between hedges, eventually climbing to a T-junction of bridlepaths in woodland. Turn right, with views across Torbay right. Cross a stile and follow the right edge of a field, with wonderful views up the Dart towards Dartmoor. Drop to a gate at a footpath junction at Higher Greenway; turn right along a rough track to meet a lane.

3 Turn left on a public right of way, passing a sign to Maypool Park (private). Pass Maypool House and follow a wooded track ahead. Pass through a gate into parkland and continue, with views left to Dartmouth.

4 Just past a bench turn right to Greenway Gardens, through two bridlegates. Keep along the right edge of a huge field, with views across the Dart to Dittisham. Pass a path junction and bear left, with trees right. Descend very steeply, soon bearing right downhill towards a gate by the car park. Turn left to a footpath junction (Greenway House left); turn right along the drive to the lane (Greenway Quay left).

5 Turn right along the little-used lane, passing Hunterswood Cottage.

6 Soon after turn left over a stone stile; follow the right field edge to cross another onto a track at Lower Greenway Farm. Bear right, then left between the farmhouse and barns. Cross a stile; head down the right edge of the field. Pass through a gate by a yellow-topped post in the wire fence; follow the fence downhill towards Galmpton Creek. At the bottom pass another post and cross a stile onto the foreshore (note the lime kiln left). For the alternative high-water route: keep ahead up the lane for 250yds (229m) to a junction of paths (Galmpton View) above Greenway Tunnel; turn left through a gate and walk downhill, aiming for a footpath post by a stream at the bottom of the field. Cross the stream and bear left towards a gate into woodland; follow the path (Hook Lane) uphill to meet the main route between Points **7** and **8**; keep ahead.

7 Turn right along the foreshore below Old Mill Farm, soon turning right up steps; turn left on a narrow tarmac way. Where a footpath to Galmpton keeps straight ahead stay on the lane as it bears right uphill, soon bearing sharp left at Hook Lane. The lane reaches Greenway Road.

8 Turn left to climb past the Galmpton village sign, then descend to the start.

DARTMOUTH AND A SPECTACULAR CASTLE

An easy round along the cliffs to Blackstone Point and Dartmouth Castle – and a ferry ride to the pub.

Dartmouth seems to have everything. The town has a rich and illustrious history and, with its smaller sister Kingswear on the opposite shore, occupies a commanding position on the banks of the Dart. With its sheltered, deep-water harbour it developed as a thriving port and shipbuilding town from the 12th century. By the 14th century it enjoyed a flourishing wine trade, and benefited from the profits of piracy for generations. Thomas Newcomen, who produced the first industrial steam engine, was born here in 1663. Today pleasure craft and the tourist industry have taken over in a big way – the annual Royal Regatta has been a major event since 1822.

Defended River Mouth

Now cared for by English Heritage, 15th-century Dartmouth Castle enjoys a beautiful position at the mouth of the Dart. Replacing the 1388 fortalice of John Hawley, it was one of the most advanced fortresses of the day and, with Kingswear Castle opposite was built to protect the homes and warehouses of the town's wealthy merchants. A chain was slung across the river mouth between the two fortifications, and guns fired from ports in the castle walls. Visitors can experience a representation of life in the later Victorian gun battery that was established. A record of 1192 infers that there was a monastic foundation on the site, leading to the establishment of St Petrock's Church, rebuilt in Gothic style within the castle precincts in 1641–42.

The cobbled quayside at Bayard's Cove, with its attractive and prosperous 17th- and 18th-century buildings (including the Customs House from 1739) was used during filming of the BBC TV series *The Onedin Line* in the 1970s. The wooded estuary a little upriver was also used for a scene supposedly set in 18th-century China, but filming was unwittingly thwarted by the sound of a steam train chuffing through the trees.

The single-storey artillery fort at Bayard's Cove was built before 1534 to protect the harbour. You can still see the gunports and the remains of a stairway leading to a walled walk above. A plaque commemorates the sailing of the *Mayflower* and *Speedwell* from the quay in 1620.

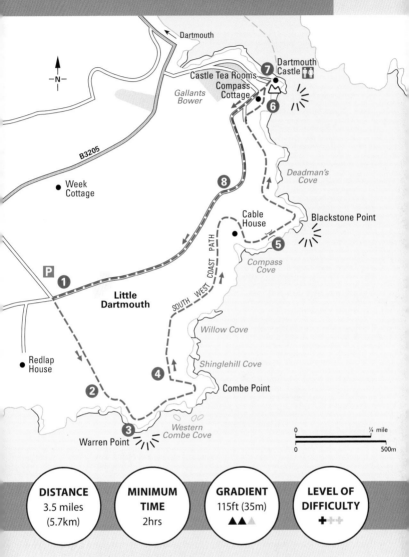

DISTANCE	MINIMUM TIME	GRADIENT	LEVEL OF DIFFICULTY
3.5 miles (5.7km)	2hrs	115ft (35m) ▲▲▲	+++

PATHS Easy coastal footpath and green lanes, 1 stile
LANDSCAPE Farmland, cliff tops and river estuary
SUGGESTED MAP OS Explorer OL20 South Devon
START/FINISH Grid reference: SX 874491
DOG FRIENDLINESS Livestock in some fields; on lead at Little Dartmouth
PARKING National Trust car parks at Little Dartmouth
PUBLIC TOILETS Dartmouth Castle

Opposite: Looking over Dartsmouth to Kingswear

WALK 11 DIRECTIONS

❶ The car parks at Little Dartmouth are signposted off the B3205. Go through the right-hand car park, following the signs 'Coast Path Dartmouth'. Continue through a kissing gate, keeping the hedge right. Walk through the next field, then through a gate and a kissing gate to join the coast path.

❷ Turn left. The coast path runs a little inland from the cliff edge, but you can always walk out on to Warren Point.

❸ From Warren Point follow the coast to pass above Western Combe Cove (with steps down to the sea) and then Combe Point (take care – it's a long drop to the sea from here).

❹ Rejoin the coast path through an open gateway in a wall and follow it above Shinglehill Cove. The path turns inland, passes a pond and follows a track, then bears right along the back of Willow Cove. It passes above woods (with a field left) and then climbs to pass through a gate. Follow the yellow arrow ahead to reach a footpath post, then turn sharp right down the valley, bearing right at the bottom to a stile

as signed. Follow the path on, and through a gate near Compass Cove.

❺ Follow the coast path left over a footbridge, and continue towards Blackstone Point. The path turns inland to run along the side of the estuary through deciduous woodland.

❻ The path meets a surfaced lane opposite Compass Cottage; keep ahead on to the lane and immediately right again steeply downhill. Follow coast path signs right to zig-zag steeply down then up steps to reach a turning space, then go right down steps to reach the castle and café.

❼ Retrace your route up the steps, then turn left up the lane to Point 6, then left to pass Compass Cottage, and continue straight on up the steep lane (signposted 'Little Dartmouth') and through a kissing gate on to National Trust land.

❽ The path runs along the top of a field and through a five-bar gate on to a green lane. Go through a gate and the farmyard at Little Dartmouth and ahead on a tarmac lane to the car park.

🍴 EATING AND DRINKING

There's the Castle Tea Rooms at Dartmouth Castle and eating places in Dartmouth – including delicious prawn sandwiches from the Crab Shell sandwich bar in Raleigh Street. Check out The Dartmouth Ice Cream Company in Duke Street. Dartmouth's oldest building, dating from c1380, today houses The Cherub pub (Higher Street). The Royal Castle Hotel overlooking the Boat Float is a free house, with good food, as is the Dartmouth Arms at historic Bayard's Cove.

SANDFORD AND UPTON HELLIONS

A gentle ramble through Mid Devon's red-earthed farmland to a delightful 12th-century church.

Sandford is a quintessential Devon village: thatched cottages, 14th-century church, excellent pub and wonderful community shop and post office, manned largely by volunteers (the average age of the newspaper delivery team was at one time over 65!). Sandford sits within a network of footpaths and green lanes that weave their way through rolling pasture fields and woodland around the valley of the Creedy, which joins the Exe just north of Exeter. The name Sandford (from 'sandy ford') predates the Norman Conquest, and the village is thought to have Saxon origins (6th or 7th century). In a charter dated AD 930 King Athelstan granted land at Sandford to Bishop Eadulf and the clergy of the minster church at Crediton. There are a number of fine houses in the parish; the original house at Creedy Park dated from about 1600, and parts of Dowrich House date from the 15th century. Sandford's particularly splendid primary school is located opposite the church, a large classical building erected in 1825 by Sir Humphrey Phineas Davie of Creedy Park.

St Mary's Church

The walk visits the little hamlet of Upton Hellions, where the simple church of St Mary's overlooks the Creedy Valley. Now only used at the great festivals, the church, which has a flagstone floor and box pews and a wonderfully unsophisticated feel, dates from the 12th century. Look out for the unusual monument of two figures kneeling at a prayer desk, said to be Richard Reynell of Creedy Widger (now Lower Creedy, passed later on the walk) and his wife Mary, who died in the mid-17th century.

The Tarka Line

If you have time, take a ride from Crediton Station on the Tarka Line, along the route of the old Exeter and Crediton Railway, which opened in 1851 and was extended to Barnstaple by the North Devon Railway three years later. You'll get a real feel of Devon's rural heartland, plus opportunities for circular walks from stations along the line, or to walk from one station to the next.

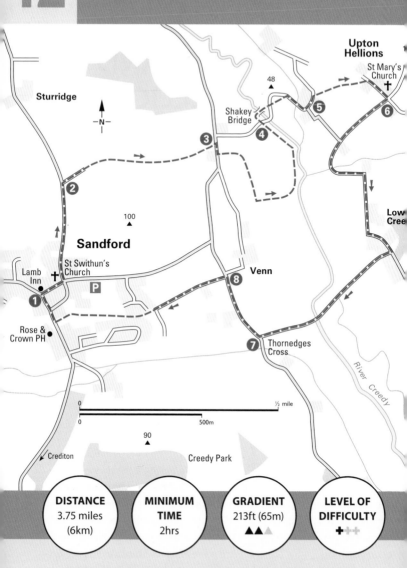

DISTANCE	MINIMUM TIME	GRADIENT	LEVEL OF DIFFICULTY
3.75 miles (6km)	2hrs	213ft (65m) ▲▲▲	✚✚✚

PATHS Rough fields, tracks, quiet lanes; muddy stretches near Creedy after wet weather, 1 stile **LANDSCAPE** Rolling farmland

SUGGESTED MAP OS Explorer 114 Exeter & the Exe Valley

START/FINISH Grid reference: SS 828025

DOG FRIENDLINESS On lead through farmland

PARKING Laneside or parish hall car park, Sandford (free)

PUBLIC TOILETS None on route, nearest at Crediton

WALK 12 DIRECTIONS

1 The walk starts from the Lamb Inn. Facing The Square turn left up Church Street past St Swithun's Church. On meeting Back Lane turn left, soon passing the primary school and follow the lane uphill out of the village.

2 Where the lane levels turn right at a footpath sign down a hedged path with a plantation left. Descend to a stile into a field, walk straight across and through a gate. Keep along the right edge of the next field, and through another; continue in the same direction and through a gate on to a lane.

3 Turn right uphill. After a few paces turn left through a gate into a field. Follow the permissive path left, turning right at the field end then right again, keeping the hedge left. At the end turn left through a gate and along the right edge of the next field to pass through a gate to meet the river. Turn left past the weir, soon crossing a stream. Follow the path ahead through a gate on to a track, with the river right.

4 Keep ahead as signed to cross the Creedy on 'Shakey Bridge' (slippery when wet). Cross a grassy area to meet a track; turn right through a gate. Head across the field, aiming to the right of the converted Hellions Mill; a mill is said to have existed here since the 13th or 14th centuries. Pass through a gate then turn right past the building to meet the lane.

5 Turn left for a few paces, then right through a gate into a field; follow the fence uphill, soon passing through a gate; continue in the same direction. At the top turn right, with a garden wall left, to pass through a gate. Keep ahead along the drive then the lane to St Mary's Church (slippery cobbles).

> ### 🍴 EATING AND DRINKING
> The popular Lamb Inn is a 16th-century posting house with accommodation, good food and a lovely garden. Make sure you try award-winning Barney's Cider, made from cider apples grown in Sandford (CAMRA's Champion Cider of Great Britain 2010). For delicious home-made cakes and a touch of railway nostalgia visit Crediton Station Tea Rooms.

6 Follow the lane that bears right downhill, later climbing to a junction at Lower Creedy (dating from Domesday). Turn right downhill to cross the Creedy.

7 At the T-junction (Thornedges Cross) turn right uphill past Mooracre Farmhouse.

8 A few paces later, opposite farm buildings, turn left on a footpath. Follow the lane through a gate into a field, soon passing through a gated/fenced section with houses right. Cross the next field and along a gated/fenced path to meet the road. Cross over to pass the post office and community stores to find the Lamb Inn.

THE TORQUAY RESERVOIRS

A peaceful excursion – wonderful with autumn colour – along the banks of two Dartmoor reservoirs.

Anyone exploring the narrow hedged lanes that thread the ridge between the Teign and Wray valleys on the eastern edge of Dartmoor may be forgiven for expressing surprise when happening upon three linked expanses of open water, fringed by oak, sweet chestnut and rhododendron. These are the Torquay Reservoirs, built between 1861 and 1907. Today the banks of these tranquil waters provide easy walking routes, and three circular options are shown on the information board at Bullaton Cross car park. Our route, however, incorporates a number of permissive paths, and can be shortened at Points ❸ and ❺ if required.

Building the Reservoirs

The dam for Kennick was constructed by Henry Brunel, son of the great 19th-century engineer Isambard Kingdom Brunel, architect of the Great Western Railway and hugely influential in the West Country. The arrival of the railway was the root cause of Torquay's development from a small fishing village into a seaside resort, and as a result the demand for water rose considerably. Tottiford was started in 1861, and soon extended; Kennick was built between 1881 and 1884 to supply the growing populations of both Torquay and Newton Abbot. In 1901 a serious drought led to the building of another dam at Trenchford, started in 1903 and completed in 1907. At times of low water parts of old Kennick Farm can be seen in the highest reservoir; to the east lie the remains of Clampitt farmhouse (occupied in the 17th century by one Elias Tuckett, a devout Quaker) and a Quaker burial ground.

More Walking and Cycling Opportunities

The popular Haldon Forest Park on nearby Haldon Hill offers walking and cycling routes. Those looking for peace and quiet should visit Haldon Belvedere (Lawrence Castle), a triangular tower built in 1788 by Sir Robert Palk in memory of Major General Stringer Lawrence, founder of the Indian Army (open Sundays and Bank Holidays February to end October). The 360 degree views from the tower are outstanding.

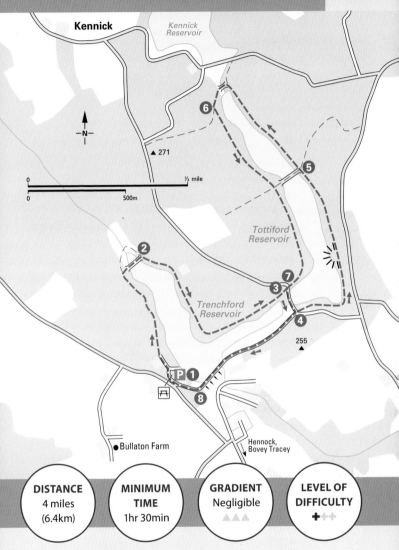

DISTANCE
4 miles
(6.4km)

MINIMUM TIME
1hr 30min

GRADIENT
Negligible
▲▲▲

LEVEL OF DIFFICULTY
✚✚✚

PATHS Raised lakeside paths, some narrow and uneven

LANDSCAPE Reservoir and woodland

SUGGESTED MAP OS Explorer 110 Torquay & Dawlish

START/FINISH Grid reference: SX 804824

DOG FRIENDLINESS On lead at all times (wildfowl)

PARKING Bullaton Cross car park (free)

PUBLIC TOILETS None on route

WALK 13 DIRECTIONS

❶ Pass the information board and follow the path into woodland. Descend towards the reservoir (rooty and muddy in places) and cross a boardwalk, and later another towards the end of the water. Bear right to cross Trenchford stream on a bridge.

❷ At the T-junction of paths turn right and follow the narrow path along the bank. Cross three boardwalks: the dam comes into view ahead. Eventually pass a beautiful stand of beech and go through a gate on to the lane.

❸ Turn right across the dam of Tottiford reservoir (to shorten the walk follow the lane back to the car park), with views right to Trendlebeare Down on Dartmoor. Old Tottiford Mill, situated just below the dam, was demolished in the early 20th century.

❹ Where the lane bears right on the other side turn left on a lane. Opposite a parking area (right) bear left past picnic tables under tall conifers on a permissive footpath. Follow another narrow raised path along the edge of Tottiford Reservoir, with open views.

❺ At a bridge and path junction keep straight on. Eventually the path broadens and becomes grassy, under oak and sweet chestnut trees. On approaching the dam for Kennick reservoir duck under rhododendron bushes and bear left past a post with a green arrow. Cross the feeder stream on a footbridge. (Fishing for rainbow trout occurs on Kennick, and the lakeside paths are closed to walkers.)

❻ On meeting a path on the other side at a post turn left along the west bank of the reservoir (note occasional forestry operations in this area). Pass a footpath junction at the bridge and keep ahead past a small wooden shelter. Follow the path back to pass through a gate on to a lane.

❼ Either cross over and retrace your steps along shores of Trenchford or, to continue on the route, turn left across the dam and follow the quiet lane, which bears right and eventually crosses the Trenchford dam: note the impressive banks of rhododendrons. A memorial stone records the start of building on 1 October 1903, and its opening four years later.

❽ Just over the dam turn right through a gate to pass the intake pipe from Fernworthy Reservoir. Pass the picnic area and ascend steps to the car park.

🍴 EATING AND DRINKING

In the mid-17th century five men were licensed to sell alcohol in the village of Hennock. Today there's just The Palk Arms, a 16th-century freehouse with wonderful views east over the Teign Valley towards the Haldon Hills and Haldon Belvedere, once owned by the Palk family, wealthy landowners.

GATEWAY TO THE MOOR

The River Bovey woodlands and the old Newton Abbot-to-Moretonhampstead railway line.

The road signs as you approach Bovey Tracey proudly proclaim the town as being the 'Gateway to the Moor', and although this may be debatable (the town is 3 miles/4.8km from the open moor, and gives no impression of Dartmoor proper) it is certainly true that the character of the landscape changes markedly as you leave the town. To the west the road climbs steadily up towards the tourist honeypot of Hay Tor, and the northern route travels past picturesque Lustleigh through the wooded Wray valley to reach Moretonhampstead and the open moorland beyond. The town's other claim to fame is that it is home to the headquarters of the Dartmoor National Park Authority, based at Parke, a splendid house set in spacious parkland to the west of the town. The River Bovey runs through the National Trust's Parke Estate, and the area provides a range of walking opportunities.

Rails to Trails

The 12-mile (19.3km) Newton Abbot–to–Moretonhampstead railway line opened in 1866, and finally closed to railway traffic in 1959. In spring 2011, part of the route near Moretonhampstead was reopened as the Wray Valley Trail for walkers, cyclists and horse riders, and there are plans to extend the line to Bovey Tracey.

Parke Estate

The building housing the National Park's offices at Parke was built around 1826 on the site of a derelict Tudor house, and left to the National Trust by Major Hole in 1974. In 1999 the National Parks of England and Wales celebrated the 50th anniversary of the legislation that established them. The Dartmoor National Park, covering 368sq miles (953sq km), was number four (in October 1951), following the Peak District, the Lake District and Snowdonia. The purpose behind the National Parks movement is 'the conservation of the natural beauty, wildlife and cultural heritage of the area, and the promotion of the understanding and enjoyment of its special qualities by the public'.

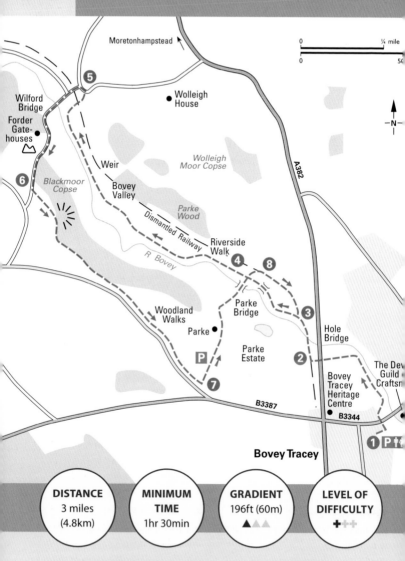

Moretonhampstead ↑

0 — ¼ mile
0 — 50

—N—

Wilford Bridge
Forder Gate-houses ⌂

Wolleigh House ●

Wolleigh Moor Copse

A382

Weir
Blackmoor Copse
Bovey Valley

Dismantled Railway

Parke Wood

Riverside Walk

R Bovey

Woodland Walks

Parke ●

Parke Bridge

Parke Estate

Hole Bridge

The Dev Guild Craftsn

Bovey Tracey Heritage Centre

B3387

B3344

Bovey Tracey

DISTANCE	MINIMUM TIME	GRADIENT	LEVEL OF DIFFICULTY
3 miles (4.8km)	1hr 30min	196ft (60m) ▲▲▲	✚✚✚

PATHS Woodland and field paths, some muddy, 2 stiles
LANDSCAPE Wooded river valley and parkland
SUGGESTED MAP OS Explorer 110 Torquay & Dawlish
START/FINISH Grid reference: SX 814782
DOG FRIENDLINESS Dogs should be kept under control at all times
PARKING Car park on the B3344 at lower end of Fore Street, Bovey Tracey, with tourist information office (seasonal) **PUBLIC TOILETS** At car park

WALK 14 DIRECTIONS

❶ Cross the road and turn right, following the signs for 'Town centre shops'. Just before you come to the bridge turn left along a walkway into Mill Marsh Park, past the playground and through the arboretum. This level footpath leads past the sports field to meet the busy A382 at Hole Bridge via a kissing gate. Cross the road carefully.

❷ Go through the kissing gate and turn right to the Parke Estate on the old trackbed of the Newton Abbot-to-Moretonhampstead railway line. Follow the path over the Bovey.

❸ Turn immediately left down steps and through a kissing gate to follow the river. Cross a stile at the field end and continue on a narrow, rough path, high above the river. Descend steps; cross a footbridge into the next field.

❹ Parke is over the bridge to the left, and the old railway line is right, but keep ahead through the field into woodland, then go left on a raised walkway to the river. The path winds on, then runs along between woods with fields on the right, then over a footbridge to meet the river at a weir. Keep following the river; eventually two kissing gates lead out of National Trust land. Keep ahead to pass a footbridge over the river left. A little later the footpath bears right to cross the railway track. Turn half left downhill to a lane via a small gate.

❺ Turn left (signed 'Manaton') and pass between the old railway bridge piers. Walk across Wilford Bridge, ignoring signs to Lustleigh, right. Continue up the lane past Forder gatehouses, right, then go steeply uphill until the lane bends sharp right.

> ### 🍴 EATING AND DRINKING
> Bovey Tracey has a number of pubs and cafés. Try The Terrace Café at The Devon Guild of Craftsmen, which serves a range of food and drink and has a lovely rooftop seating area, or – just down the road – Brookside, a licensed café and tea garden.

❻ Turn left over a stile to re-enter the Parke Estate. Go through a beech wood and kissing gate to enter a large field. Keep to the right edge, dropping gradually downhill, to leave via a kissing gate and down a narrow wooded path parallel to the road.

❼ The path ends at a kissing gate; turn sharp left to walk across the parkland and the drive to Parke car park. Walk downhill to cross the lower drive, then left to go below the house, ending at a five-bar gate. Go through and turn right ('Riverside Walk') to cross the river at Parke Bridge, then ahead to join the old railway track.

❽ Turn right and follow the track until it crosses the Bovey, to meet the A382. Cross the road to enter Mill Marsh Park and retrace your steps to your car.

ST MARY'S CHURCH AND MOLLAND COMMON

Look out for red deer and Exmoor ponies on this hilly walk that clips the edge of Molland Common.

If you approach South Molton via the Chulmleigh road, which heads north through beautiful rolling farmland, the town known as 'the gateway to Exmoor' suddenly appears against a wonderful backdrop of Exmoor's southernmost hills.

Granted a market charter and the right to hold an annual fair (still celebrated in June) in 1357, it still has an active pannier market and main weekly market. The undulating farmland around the town is some of the least walked in the county, yet home to a wealth of small villages, hamlets and scattered farmsteads, linked by a labyrinth of narrow lanes.

St Mary's Church and the Molland Lily

One particularly interesting settlement is Molland, nestled in unspoiled countryside between the A361 and Exmoor 7.5 miles (12.1km) east of South Molton. This tiny village shelters beneath the swell of Molland Common, surrounded by hilly farmland and wooded combes. It is home to a good pub, a tea room and – most significantly – the most perfect example of a Georgian church found in Devon. St Mary's Church escaped the attentions of Victorian restorers: step through the enormously heavy wooden door (the weight of which in itself implies you have arrived somewhere special) and you are met by dark high box pews, flagstone floors, ornate 17th- and 18th-century monuments to the Courtenay family who lived at West Molland, leaning arcades and an impressive three-decker canopied pulpit. During conservation work in 2009 a section of the original seating dating from 1500 was found partially supporting the pulpit; the existing box pews date from the early 18th century. In the church you will also find information relating to the Molland lily, rare in the country and thought to have been introduced to North Devon by monks from Spain in medieval times.

You'll see Exmoor ponies on Molland Common and are also quite likely to see some of Exmoor's famed red deer, the largest wild animal in England. Exmoor was once a Royal Forest, and the red deer population was hunted for venison. Today there are around 3,000 animals on the moor.

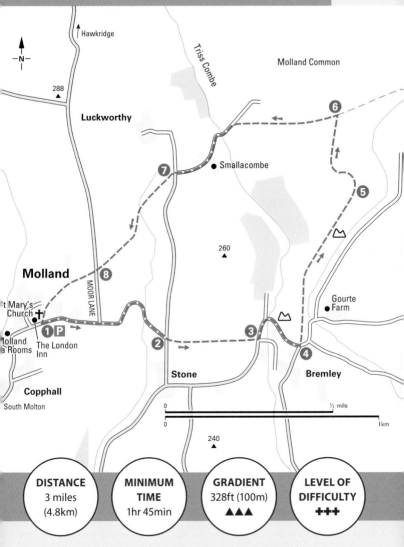

DISTANCE
3 miles (4.8km)

MINIMUM TIME
1hr 45min

GRADIENT
328ft (100m) ▲▲▲

LEVEL OF DIFFICULTY
+++

PATHS Field paths and moorland tracks (some muddy after wet weather), steep ascent to Molland Common, 2 stiles **LANDSCAPE** Farmland and moorland

SUGGESTED MAP OS Explorer OL9 Exmoor

START/FINISH Grid reference: SS 808284

DOG FRIENDLINESS Under control at all times; on lead in nesting season (1 March–15 July) and in churchyard

PARKING Near St Mary's Church, Molland **PUBLIC TOILETS** None on route

WALK 15 DIRECTIONS

❶ With the church left follow the lane away from The London Inn. Where it bears sharp left (Moor Lane), by a disused chapel, keep straight on, dropping steeply into and out of a combe to reach Latchgate Cross; the lane bears sharp right.

❷ Keep ahead, turning right through a gate. Turn left along the top edge of two fields via gates. At the end of a third, cross a stile; the ground ahead drops steeply. Pick your way down through a gully and turn left; a few paces later turn right downhill to cross a stile on to the lane.

❸ Turn left, immediately curving right to climb steeply. The lane reaches Bremley Cross.

❹ Ignore bridleway signs ahead; immediately turn left towards a signed gate. Follow the track up the west side of a combe, with Gourte Farm right. The track bears right away from the hedge bank and climbs steeply (good views to Dartmoor behind). The wide-open spaces of Molland Common appear invitingly ahead. Eventually follow the track left through a gate.

❺ Keep along the left edge of the field. Turn right at the corner; about 100yds (91m) before the field end bear slightly left to pass through a gate on to Molland Common.

❻ Turn left along the lower edge, soon descending, with a hedge bank left. The track becomes more defined; at a bridleway post follow the track right then left to cross a small ford and footbridge over a stream. Pass through a gate; follow the hedged track uphill past Smallacombe Farm.

❼ At a T-junction keep ahead through a signed gate into a field. Cross diagonally, passing to the right of a fence corner, then through a gate in the field corner. Keep straight ahead, dropping steeply over a disused leat to a footbridge/stile/footbridge; ascend steps onto a grassy track. Turn left; where the track forks keep ahead, uphill, passing a line of beech trees. Cross the field in the same direction, and through a gate on to Moor Lane.

> **🍴 EATING AND DRINKING**
> Molland Tea Rooms (seasonal; open from Easter to October), serves home-made cakes and can provide lots of local information. The London Inn, a 15th-century coaching inn, is a traditional country pub.

❽ Cross over and through a gate. Cross the field to pass through a gate. Head across the next, dropping through a gate on to a track; keep ahead downhill to the left of farm buildings. After a few paces turn left into the churchyard; soon turn left for the church, or right, then left and left again for your car.

ASHTON CLEAVE AND THE OARE WATER

A county-border walk from one of Exmoor's finest viewpoints, with an optional extension into 'Doone Country'.

This superb walk starts on the Devon–Somerset border and trips in and out of the two counties. From the start the views down the steep-sided valleys of the East Lyn and ahead up the Badgworthy Water towards the heart of the moor are breathtaking.

This is a great walk for giving you a real 'feel' of Exmoor, and along the sparkling East Lyn river you will be tempted to sit down and while away an hour or two in idyllic surroundings.

The Doone Valley

Whereas many have heard the name 'Lorna Doone', few realise that the valley of the Badgworthy Water runs through what is commonly known as 'Doone Country' on account of its links with R D Blackmore's novel of the same name, published in 1869. In the story Lorna was kidnapped by the Doones, a notorious family of outlaws said to live in Hoccombe Combe, a tributary valley. An easy 3-mile (4.8km) walk south along the river from Malmsmead leads to the site.

From 1809 to 1842 Blackmore's grandfather was rector of the 1,000-year-old St Mary's Church at Oare, under a mile (1.6km) to the east of Malmsmead, and it is likely that R D would have add access to parish records: he frequently uses local place-names in his novel, and at times it is hard to distinguish fact from fiction. Lorna was shot on the day of her wedding to Jan Ridd, and Blackmore is thought to have taken this scene from the sad (true) story of Mary Whiddon in Chagford who was shot in 1641.

Evidence of Roman Occupation

Remains of a Roman outpost/fortlet have been found on Old Burrow Hill, just north of Cosgate Hill (passed on Point ❶). Excavations have revealed well-preserved banks that would have originally contained tented accommodation for around 60 men. Ancient burial mounds have also been identified on Cosgate and nearby hills.

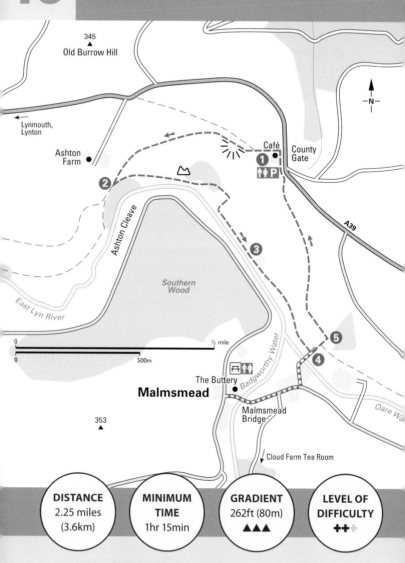

DISTANCE	MINIMUM TIME	GRADIENT	LEVEL OF DIFFICULTY
2.25 miles (3.6km)	1hr 15min	262ft (80m) ▲▲▲	++

PATHS Narrow moorland paths, uneven riverside path, steep final ascent

LANDSCAPE Moorland and river valley

SUGGESTED MAP OS Explorer OL9 Exmoor

START/FINISH Grid reference: SS 793486

DOG FRIENDLINESS Under control at all times; on lead in nesting season (1 March–15 July) and at Point ❸

PARKING County Gate car park (free) **PUBLIC TOILETS** County Gate car park

WALK 16 DIRECTIONS

❶ Walk towards the far right corner of the car park, past the toilets, to a footpath post by the John Peel Memorial. Take the left fork, signed 'Brendon', enjoying spectacular views over steep-sided Ashton Cleave and beyond to Brendon Common and Exmoor's highest ground, The Chains (rising to just under 1,600ft/487m). Follow the narrow path above Ashton Cleave, eventually dropping to a footpath post just before a gate.

🍴 EATING AND DRINKING

The Buttery tea room and licensed bar next to Malmsmead Bridge has a pretty garden and sells good local ice cream. There's also the County Gate café and local information point by the car park, and another tea room at Cloud Farm in the Doone Valley.

---

❷ Turn sharp left downhill, signed 'Malmsead and Oare'. The path descends steeply along the top edge of pretty oak and birch woodland to meet the East Lyn River, and continues along its left bank. Pass through a kissing gate and along the right edge of a small meadow, then through a big gate between a high hedge and the river.

❸ Pass through a gate by a white cottage (private: note there is no access to the lane here, and dogs should be kept on leads), cross the drive and through another gate.

The broad grassy path passes the confluence of the Oare and Badgworthy waters; follow the Oare Water ahead.

❹ Reach a big footbridge over the river. For the optional 0.5-mile (800m) there-and-back extension to Malmsmead, cross the footbridge and follow the path gently uphill and through a gate to a lane. Turn right to pass the drive to Cloud Farm, soon crossing 17th-century Malmsmead Bridge over the Badgworthy Water. To continue on the main the walk pass the footbridge, soon turning left away from the river and ascending gently past a bridlepath sign.

❺ At the next sign turn left and climb steadily uphill through gorse and bracken, eventually to pass through a gate into the car park. A dilapidated wall running down the valley side to the left marks the Devon–Somerset border. Look out also for areas of scree on the steep valley sides, resulting from intense freeze-thaw action in the underlying rock.

🌀 IN THE AREA

Take a trip on the amazing Cliff Railway, an easy route up (or down) the 900ft (275m) cliffs between Lynmouth and Lynton. Constructed in 1890, and powered by water, the railway was at the time the steepest of its kind in the world, with a gradient of 1 in 1.75.

View of Ashton Cleave from Cosgate Hill.

THE DEEP SOUTH AT PRAWLE POINT

A land of shipwrecks and smugglers, gannets and skuas, and some of the oldest rocks in Devon.

It seems to take forever to get to East Prawle. This secluded spit is completely unspoilt, and popular with Devon people who want a simple camping holiday. Prawle Point, just below the village, is the most southerly point in Devon. The easiest way to get there is by car, but it's far more satisfying to submit to the sleepy atmosphere and wander down the lanes and along the coast, past some of the most beautiful coves in Devon.

Lookout Point

The lookout at Prawle Point is today manned on a voluntary basis to keep an eye on this particularly busy part of the coast. Originally a coastguard station, with a 270-degree field of vision, it was used by Lloyds of London to report the arrival of ships from across the Atlantic. In use as a naval signal service station from 1937 to 1940, it shut down as a coastguard station in 1994. Prawle means 'lookout hill', so this practice could date back to Saxon times.

Prawle Point is home to a great variety of birds and, due to its southerly position, is visited by a wealth of early and rare varieties on spring and autumn migrations. Birders can usually see a full range of gulls, kestrels, cormorants, common terns, skylarks and common buzzards as well as gannets and great skuas (this is an internationally important habitat for these two species). The rare and localised cirl bunting is also a resident here – there were only 80 pairs in the country in 1989, but successful conservation measures have lead to a considerable increase in numbers.

Devon's Oldest Rocks

The volcanic rocks of the coast here are some of Devon's oldest, dating back over 400 million years. Pressure from the earth's movements split the strata and realigned them into parallel bands. The pounding sea then created the split, angular rocks evident today. The raised beach below East Prawle, a distinctive platform 15ft (4.5m) above the present beach, was formed during the last two million years in times of warmer weather conditions and higher sea levels, which altered coastal erosion patterns.

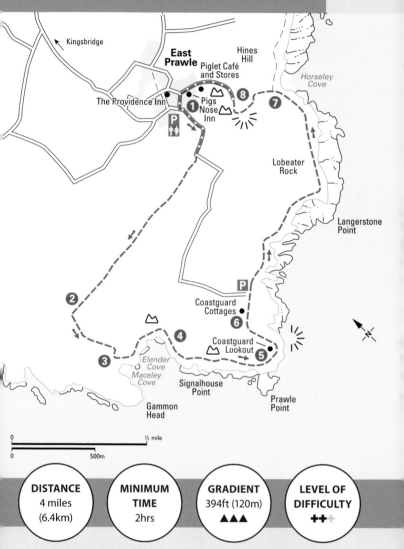

DISTANCE
4 miles
(6.4km)

MINIMUM
TIME
2hrs

GRADIENT
394ft (120m)
▲▲▲

LEVEL OF
DIFFICULTY
++╋

PATHS Green lanes, fields and coast path, rocky in places, 2 stiles
LANDSCAPE Coastal farmland, rocky coves and level raised beaches
SUGGESTED MAP OS Explorer OL20 South Devon
START/FINISH Grid reference: SX 780363
DOG FRIENDLINESS Dogs to be kept under control at all times
PARKING Around green in East Prawle (honesty box contributions)
PUBLIC TOILETS By green in East Prawle

Walk 17 — East Prawle

WALK 17 DIRECTIONS

❶ Walk down the lane towards the sea, leaving the green to the left and toilets and a phone box right and following a sign 'Prawle Point'. After a few minutes the lane turns sharp left; go straight ahead along a deeply rutted green lane marked 'Public Bridleway'.

❷ The green lane ends at a T-junction (metal gates opposite); turn left down a very narrow grassy path between tumbledown, overgrown old walls. There are fine views of the coast ahead. Follow the path through a kissing gate to the footpath post.

❸ Turn right downhill to the coast path high above secluded Maceley Cove, with Gammon Head to the right. Turn left and walk along the path above Elender Cove. There is steep, scrambly access to both beaches but take care.

❹ The path leads through a kissing gate and scrambles on around Signalhouse Point. A steep ascent, partly stepped, is rewarded with fine views ahead to the wreck of the *Demetrios* on the rocks, with Prawle Point beyond. Follow the footpath posts through a gate and across the grassy down, keeping to the right of the coastguard lookout ahead.

❺ At the coastguard lookout enjoy superb views east and explore the excellent visitor centre. To continue, follow the grassy path inland, rejoining the coast path, and head towards the old coastguard cottages.

❻ Turn right through a kissing gate to pass in front of the cottages and along the edge of the level, grassy wavecut platform which lies just below the original Pleistocene cliffs here. Pass through a gate (note a parking area across the field to the left) and along lovely level meadows above low cliffs. Go through the next kissing gate. The next gate leads on to Langerstone Point. Continue round field-edges and through another gate; Maelcombe House is now in sight ahead. Pass through two more gates and keep ahead to a path junction.

❼ Turn left up the bridleway; eventually pass through a gate and keep ahead up the track.

❽ Take the first stile right to go very steeply up the field. There are good views back to the coast. Cross the stile at the top and continue right up the rocky track to join the lane, ascending right steeply back to the village.

> ### 🍴 EATING AND DRINKING
> East Prawle is blessed with two good pubs. The 18th-century Providence Inn is full of smuggling and shipwreck memorabilia. It's also very welcoming, and serves excellent food. The Pigs Nose Inn has a menu geared towards families. You can also get snacks and refreshments at the Piglet Café.

HAYTOR GRANITE TRAMWAY

Step back in time to the days when horse-drawn wagons rumbled along the Granite Tramway.

Haytor Rocks (1,499ft/457m) has been Dartmoor's most famous landmark since Victorian times, and the relatively easy walk up the slopes to the massive rocks attracts day trippers and holidaymakers all year round. But whereas the vast majority of visitors simply walk from the car park to the Rocks and back, there is a quieter and historically fascinating side to Haytor that is explored on this gentle route.

Haytor is also fortunate in that it is sited on the southern edge of the moor, overlooking one of the best arrays of tors – impressive piles of weathered granite – on Dartmoor. On leaving the quarry on Point ❹ you can see Cosdon Hill (see Walk 25) on the far northeast of the moor and, nearer, Hound Tor (left) and Smallacombe Rocks (right). In May, Holwell Lawn, towards Hound Tor, is a shimmering blue carpet of bluebells. It's an excellent route for viewing the maximum number of tors in a short distance.

George Templer's Tramway

The tramway followed on this walk was built in 1820 by George Templer (1781–1843) to service his quarries at Haytor. This hugely ambitious project was proposed to link the quarries with the head of the Stover Canal, constructed by George's father James, to carry clay from the family mines in the Bovey Basin to the sea at Teignmouth. The building of the tramway (8.5 miles (13.7km) long, with a fall of 1300ft/396m) was prompted by an order to provide stone for the British Museum and the arches of London Bridge. The 'rails' were cut from granite; teams of Shire horses hauled flatbed trucks up the tramway after the downhill run to the canal. By 1858 the quarries were no longer economic and were abandoned along with the tramway.

The Templer Way

Today the Templer family's Dartmoor heritage is celebrated by a waymarked 18-mile (29km) walking trail that follows the course of the route used to export clay and granite from Haytor to the south coast at Shaldon, opposite Teignmouth at the mouth of the River Teign.

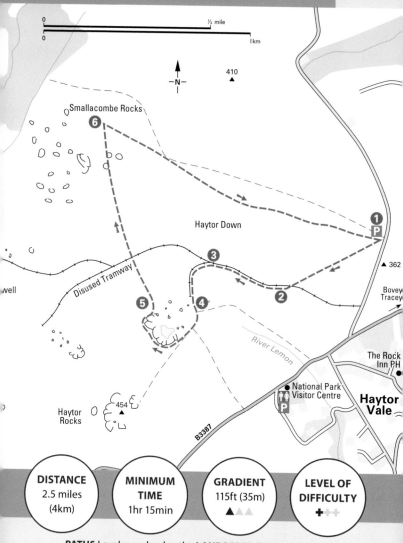

Haytor Down

Disused Tramway

Smallacombe Rocks

Haytor Rocks

454

362

410

River Lemon

The Rock Inn P.H

Haytor Vale

National Park Visitor Centre

Bovey Tracey

B3387

well

½ mile
1 km

DISTANCE
2.5 miles
(4km)

MINIMUM TIME
1hr 15min

GRADIENT
115ft (35m)
▲▲▲

LEVEL OF DIFFICULTY
✚ ✚ ✚

PATHS Level moorland paths **LANDSCAPE** Open moorland
SUGGESTED MAP OS Explorer OL9 Dartmoor
START/FINISH Grid reference: SX 770778
DOG FRIENDLINESS Under control at all times; on lead in nesting season
(1 March–15 July) **PARKING** Unmarked car park (free) on Haytor Down
PUBLIC TOILETS At bottom Haytor car park **NOTE** Do not attempt in misty
weather; numerous paths so follow directions carefully; in quarries supervise small
children and put dogs on lead

Opposite: Haytor Rocks in Dartmoor National Park

WALK 18 DIRECTIONS

❶ From the car park take a narrow path that runs between low-growing gorse in the direction of Haytor (slightly to the left of the rocks). The path drops gently, soon passing through a small gully: quarry spoil heaps soon come into view to the right of Haytor.

❷ On meeting a broader grassy path (in which you can see granite setts, marking the line of the Haytor Granite Tramway) turn right. The setts come and go, but look carefully and you will spot the odd one under grass to the right. A boggy area (left) marks the source of the River Lemon, which flows south to meet the River Teign in Newton Abbot. Look left to see Haytor Quarries.

❸ Reach an obvious set of points (junction of granite setts) and a fork in the path: bear left to follow a branch line, which curves towards the left end of the quarry. Various bumps in the ground here indicate the site of cottages and a pub built by Templer for his workers. The tramway reaches a gap between two spoil heaps (a turning area), with views ahead towards the coast.

❹ Immediately through the spoil heaps look right to spot a small gully. Immediately past that turn right up a narrow path that climbs along the left bank of the gully, soon meeting a wire fence. After 50yds (46m) turn right through a small wooden gate and follow the path past two quarry ponds, a haven of tranquillity. After the second pond, cross a stile through the outer embankment.

❺ Immediately bear left on a broad grassy path, with fine views. The path hits the tramway again, with Holwell Quarries to the left; keep ahead and slightly right, aiming for Smallacombe Rocks through low-growing gorse and heather. After 75yds (69m) meet a broader path and bear right; as the path begins to climb gently take the left fork of two paths, aiming for the right end of the rocks.

> **🍽 EATING AND DRINKING**
>
> Originally an 18th-century coaching inn, The Rock Inn at Haytor Vale sits alongside old quarrymen's cottages, and was once the single-workers' hostel. The excellent Barn Café at Ullacombe Farm Shop, just down the Bovey Tracey road, serves good home-made locally sourced food. Look out for ice cream vans in the main Haytor car parks.

❻ Once level with the rocks look right to find a broad grassy path that runs away across the horizon, midway between Haytor Rocks (right) and aptly named Hole Rock which can be seen on the horizon to the left. Turn right (east-south-east) across Haytor Down, eventually dropping to the car park with views to the coast ahead.

SALCOMBE AND EAST PORTLEMOUTH

The peaceful Kingsbridge Estuary to the west of Prawle Point
is popular with both walkers and boating folk.

Salcombe is a delightful place but incredibly popular in season, it's best to
park away from the town and approach it by ferry or on foot. Walk in along
the coast path around Bolt Head, to the west of the estuary; or follow this
walk from the tiny hamlet of East Portlemouth, opposite the town, from
where you get some of the best views in the area over the mass of small boats
in the harbour, and the various creeks upriver towards Kingsbridge.

Once the haunt of smugglers and pirates, today Salcombe has a civilised,
prosperous and – as a result of its sheltered position and deep blue waters
– an almost Mediterranean feel. The estuary is a marvellous place for young
families, too. At low tide there is a run of sandy beaches all along the East
Portlemouth side, enabling those staying in Salcombe simply to hop on the
ferry for a day on the beach. (Note: Many of these sandy coves are cut off at
high tide and there is no access from the shore – take care.)

From Limebury Point you can see across the estuary to Overbecks, an
elegant Edwardian house in a magnificent setting above South Sands. Otto
Overbeck, who lived here from 1928 to 1937, left the house and its 6-acre
(2.4ha) garden to the National Trust, and it's worth visiting for the garden
alone. There is a fantastic collection of rare and sub-tropical plants here,
thriving in the temperate conditions. The house is fun, too (there's masses to
keep children occupied). Overbeck was a collector of all manners of things,
many of which – shells, toys, model boats, shipbuilding tools – are on display.

An Interesting Past

East Portlemouth has a totally different feel to Salcombe. It is small,
very quiet and unspoilt, and somewhat belies its rather difficult history.
During the 19th century half the population was evicted by the absentee
landlord, the Duke of Cleveland, as a result of their preference for fishing and
wrecking over working the land. The 15th-century church is dedicated to
St Winwalloe, a 5th-century Celtic saint, and a fascinating gravestone in the
churchyard reveals the death by burning at the stake of a girl who poisoned
her employer in 1782.

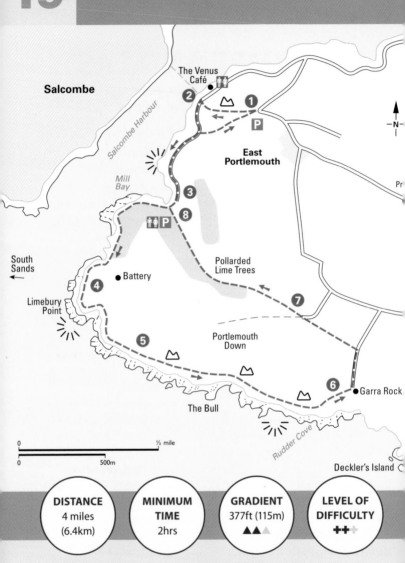

DISTANCE	MINIMUM TIME	GRADIENT	LEVEL OF DIFFICULTY
4 miles (6.4km)	2hrs	377ft (115m) ▲▲▲	++ +

PATHS Good coast path, field paths and tracks **LANDSCAPE** River estuary, rocky coast and coves, farmland **SUGGESTED MAP** OS Explorer OL20 South Devon **START/FINISH** Grid reference: SX 746386 **DOG FRIENDLINESS** Dogs to be kept under control at all times **PARKING** Near phone box in East Portlemouth or in small parking area **PUBLIC TOILETS** At Mill Bay, passed on Points ❸ and ❼, and near The Venus Café **NOTE** Many of the sandy coves on the route are cut off at high tide and there is no access from the shore

WALK 19 DIRECTIONS

❶ Park on the verge near the phone box at East Portlemouth (or in the parking area – village hall fund contributions). Go across the parking area and steeply downhill on a narrow tarmac footpath signposted 'Salcombe', which gives way to steep steps.

❷ When you reach the lane at the bottom of the steps, turn right to The Venus Café and the ferry to Salcombe. If you want to get on with the walk, turn left along the lane as it follows the edge of the estuary.

❸ The lane leads to the pretty, sandy beach at Mill Bay. Carefully follow the acorn coast path signs for Gara Rock through a sycamore wood, with lovely views across the estuary, and glimpses of inviting little coves.

❹ At Limebury Point you reach the cliff. The coast path now bears eastwards below Portlemouth Down.

❺ The path along this stretch undulates steeply, and is rocky in places. Keep going until you reach the bench and viewpoint over the beach at Rickham Sands. Just beyond this, as the coast path continues right (there is reasonable access to the beach), take the left fork and climb steeply up below the lookout to reach a signpost by the site of the old Gara Rock holiday development.

❻ Turn left to reach the hotel drive and walk up the lane. After 250yds (229m) turn left through a gate in the hedge signposted 'Mill Bay'. Walk straight ahead through a gate and across the field, bearing right to a gate; note Malborough church in the distance. Go through a small copse, then a gate and across the farm track. Go through a gate down the public bridleway.

❼ This runs gradually downhill with a grassy combe to the right. The path leads past the car park to Mill Bay.

❽ Turn right along the lane. If you want to avoid the steps, look out for a footpath sign pointing right, up a narrow, steep, path to regain East Portlemouth and your car; if not, continue along the lane and retrace your route up the steps.

🍴 EATING AND DRINKING

Salcombe has plenty of excellent pubs, cafés and restaurants to choose from, but if you want to stay on the East Portlemouth side try The Venus Café (one of a chain of extremely 'green' beach cafés). It's in a glorious position by the ferry slipway, with a pretty garden looking across the water. The café serves great food and drink, and is open every day from Easter to the end of October. The ferry to Salcombe runs daily throughout the year.

KINGSBRIDGE AND BOWCOMBE CREEK

Historic trading routes by land and sea are traced on this delightful walk with magical views over the estuary.

The best way to appreciate why the south Devon market town of Kingsbridge has such a long history of seaborne trade – evidenced by a number of fine buildings dating from wealthier times in the 18th and 19th centuries – is to climb high above town. From this walk extensive views over the many-branched estuary clearly show this long-established port's commanding position.

The Early Port

Kingsbridge has long been a centre for trade, a link between the rural hinterland and the sea. The town flourished on account of its location at the head of a 5-mile (8km) long navigable estuary at a time when transport inland was difficult and routes frequently impassable, and from medieval times – when the town enjoyed healthy trading links with south-west France – until the coming of the railway in 1893, the quays would have bustled with life. Take a look at the Shambles on Fore Street, a granite pillared walkway, formerly the site of butchers' stalls in the heart of the medieval town.

Later clippers, schooners and barges were built on the banks of the estuary, and packet steamers came to call. The advent of steel ships which could not access the higher reaches of the estuary – and the arrival of the railway – ended the town's life as a port, and it is now a popular holiday spot.

Bowcombe Creek

Just one of many creeks on the estuary, Bowcombe too has a long history of local trade. Slate from a nearby quarry, and cider from farms, was shipped out, and there was at one time a mill at the head of the creek. Today it is a haven for birds and wildlife.

Along the route, keep an eye out for wading birds on Bowcombe Creek, once site of a huge heronry; in particular herons and little egrets may be seen. Winter is a particularly good time for spotting redshanks, greenshanks, oystercatchers and curlews.

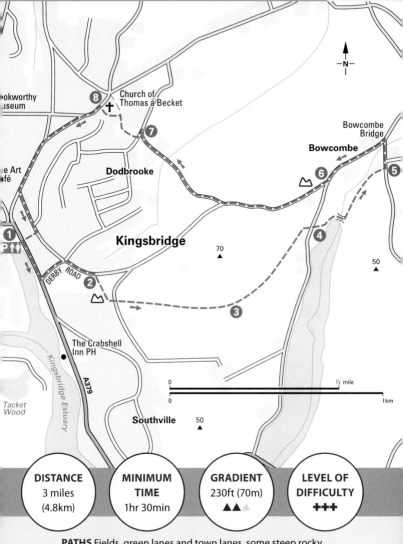

DISTANCE	MINIMUM TIME	GRADIENT	LEVEL OF DIFFICULTY
3 miles (4.8km)	1hr 30min	230ft (70m) ▲▲△	+++

PATHS Fields, green lanes and town lanes, some steep rocky
ascents/descents, at times wet underfoot in Bowcombe Creek, 6 stiles

LANDSCAPE River estuary and rolling farmland

SUGGESTED MAP OS Explorer OL20 South Devon

START/FINISH Grid reference: SX 735441

DOG FRIENDLINESS On lead, not allowed in churchyard (keep ahead along path)

PARKING Car park on Kingsbridge Quay (pay-and-display)

PUBLIC TOILETS In car park opposite the tourist information centre

WALK 20 DIRECTIONS

1 From the TIC cross the road and turn right parallel to the tidal creek. Soon turn left up Derby Road, noting Dodbrooke Lodge left, once the coach house for Dodbrooke Manor. At the first crossroads turn right down Derby Road to pass the recreation ground.

2 The lane bears left; bear right on a footpath through a gate. Ascend a very steep rough field and go through a gate on to a lane. Cross over and ascend steps on a footpath through the rugby club car park. Cross a stile; follow a fenced path up the left edge of a field. Cross a stone stile and reach a footpath junction.

3 Follow the top edge of the next field, curving left with the hedge. Cross a stile and, where the hedge bears away bear right, past a fence corner and footpath post. Continue steeply downhill, towards a gate by a derelict building. Pass through, cross a stile and bear right over another on to a lane.

4 Cross a stile ahead; the path bears left through a gate in a fence into creekside reed beds. (If you find this stretch too wet return to the lane, turn right, then left at Point **6**.) Cross the head of the creek on a bridge; turn left over a stile into a field. Keep along the bottom left edge and through a gate, with the brook left. Continue along the left edge of the next, turning right uphill at the end to a stile onto a lane.

5 Turn left downhill to cross Bowcombe Bridge; turn left along the lane to pass Bridge Park Cottage.

6 At the entrance to Tonge Field Farm turn right on a deeply banked green lane that climbs steeply before levelling off. At a fork bear right and descend steadily (rough underfoot) to reach Washabrook Mill in a sheltered combe, once a tidal mill for flour and grist. Pass Washabrook Farm and follow the lane uphill to Washabrook Lane.

7 Turn left, follow the road uphill, 25yds (23m) after passing a bridlepath (left) turn right on a tarmac path. At gates turn left into the churchyard of St Thomas à Becket; turn right, then left towards the church. Pass round the tower to emerge on to Church Street.

8 Turn left downhill. Where the road eventually kinks right bear left along Ebrington Street. Where the street broadens turn right down an alley to find the pedestrian crossing and TIC.

> **🍴 EATING AND DRINKING**
> If you're out with children take them to The Art Café on Fore Street, where you can decorate your own mug or bowl while enjoying a bowl of home-made soup or tea and cake. The Crabshell Inn on the estuary – a crab-catching hot spot – specialises in seafood, and has extensive outside seating overlooking the water.

CHAGFORD AND THE RIVER TEIGN

A popular stroll through one of Dartmoor's prettiest towns and along the banks of the Teign.

The ancient town of Chagford, situated on the north-east edge of the moor above the River Teign and in the shadow of Meldon and Nattadon commons, is justifiably one of Dartmoor's most attractive – and hence most visited – spots.

A Varied History

As early as the 12th century it developed as a market centre for the surrounding moorland, and in 1305 its importance was verified when it became one of Dartmoor's stannary towns. 'Stannary' was the name given to centres of tin assaying and taxation, and Chagford was confirmed as such by Edward I – it remained an important centre until the mid-17th century (Dartmoor's other stannary towns were Ashburton, Plympton and Tavistock). As tin returns declined, wool grew in economic importance locally, and Chagford mills spun yarns for the prosperous towns of East Devon: two are passed on this walk.

In late Victorian times the town developed as a moorland holiday resort, with visitors arriving by horse-drawn coaches from the railway at Moretonhampstead. The town's links with the tin industry are remembered today by the Tinners' Fair, held each May, and by one of the roof bosses in the church which shows the' tinners' rabbits', a well-known local symbol showing three rabbits in a circle, said to represent the many warrens that were developed on the moor to rear rabbits as food for the mining community (see Walk 28). Recent research, however, has revealed the existence of this symbol across the world, and on the Silk Route as far as China.

Annual Drift Sales

Chagford is also home to one of the annual drift sales, where ponies – all of which belong to someone – living wild on Dartmoor are rounded up and auctioned. Those unsold are micro-chipped and returned to the moor. The sale takes place in October, and is a wonderful insight into the lives of the Dartmoor Commoners.

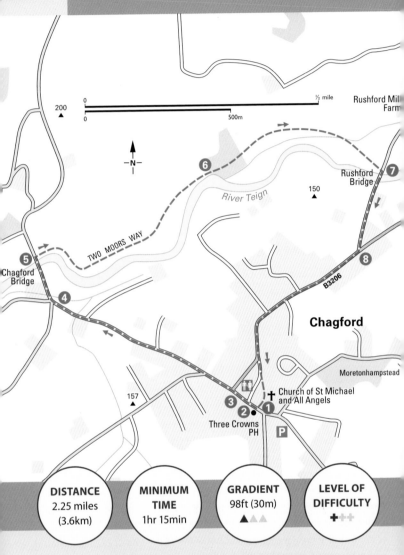

200 ▲

0 ——————————————— ½ mile

0 ——————————————— 500m

Rushford Mill Farm

—N—

⑥

River Teign

150 ▲

Rushford Bridge

⑦

TWO MOORS WAY

⑤

Chagford Bridge

④

⑧

B3206

Chagford

Moretonhampstead

157 ▲

✝ Church of St Michael and All Angels

③
②
①

Three Crowns PH

🅿

DISTANCE
2.25 miles
(3.6km)

MINIMUM TIME
1hr 15min

GRADIENT
98ft (30m)
▲ ▲ ▲

LEVEL OF DIFFICULTY
✛ ✛ ✛

PATHS Riverside path (parts muddy after wet weather) through fields, quiet lanes

LANDSCAPE Farmland, woodland and town

SUGGESTED MAP OS Explorer OL28 Dartmoor

START/FINISH Grid reference: SX 701875

DOG FRIENDLINESS On lead through farmland

PARKING Car park in Chagford (pay-and-display)

PUBLIC TOILETS The Pepperpot in The Square

WALK 21 DIRECTIONS

① The walk starts from the west end of the 15th-century Church of St Michael and All Angels, underneath the clock, at the junction of four paths. Bear half right and walk diagonally across the graveyard, noting The Globe Inn and early 16th-century Three Crowns on the left. Pass through a gate on to the High Street.

② Turn right and walk through The Square. The Pepperpot (an octagonal market house) dates from 1862, and was built by George Hayter-Hames, a local benefactor who sponsored various town improvements.

③ Pass Webbers and then Bowdens stores, extraordinary emporia crammed with every household item you can imagine: well worth an exploration after your walk, but allow plenty of time! Webbers began life in 1898; Bowdens in 1862 as the Vulcan Ironworks. Head down Mill Street. Meet a fork in the lane and keep right. The lane descends more steeply through a cutting to meet a junction at Factory Cross.

---

⑪ EATING AND DRINKING

Chagford has several pubs and cafés. Try the historic Three Crowns overlooking the churchyard; The Courtyard Organic Café & Wholefoods for mezze platters and chunky soups; and The New Forge opposite for light lunches and a range of teas.

---

④ Bear right, signed 'Gidleigh and Throwleigh'. Cross Chagford Bridge, dating from before 1224.

⑤ Once over the bridge turn right through a gate on the route of the Two Moors Way/Devon Coast to Coast. Pass through a kissing gate and pass huge oaks protected by granite collars. Pass through a gate and continue across rough grass and bracken; note the converted mill on the opposite bank. A succession of fields and gates follows to reach the weir.

⑥ At this point the path swings away from the river and follows a leat that feeds Rushford Mill, and also supplies Chagford's lovely open-air swimming pool, which celebrated its 75th birthday in 2009. Pass through gates and fields to a footpath junction; keep ahead again to cross the leat. Keep ahead across the field, with a hedge right. Pass through the hedge and bear left across the next field to reach the lane by Rushford Bridge.

⑦ Turn right across the river and follow the lane, which climbs steadily to a T-junction at Crossways.

⑧ Turn right and follow the road back into town past attractive houses and cottages. Where you see The New Forge on the left bear left. Turn left again before Blacks Delicatessen into the churchyard; keep ahead to return to the start.

THE RIVER TAW AND BOUCHERS HILL

A wonderfully varied walk, from wooded river valley to open hilltop with superb views towards the North Moor.

Situated in fertile countryside to the north of Dartmoor, the small rural town of North Tawton has long been important for wool: in times past the main product was serge, a hard-wearing cloth made from the fleece of the Devon longwool sheep. But North Tawton is also currently home to two of West Devon's largest businesses: Gregory's Transport (founded in 1919 by Archie Gregory, who hauled coal from the railway station to the wool factory by horse and cart) and the Taw Valley Creamery, both of which give the town a sense of pride and purpose.

Agricultural Memorabilia

At Bridge Farm you will see an unrestored roundhouse, originally built to house the werewithal for threshing the grain from the chaff. A horse would have been harnessed to a central beam and walked round and round to operate the machinery. Such roundhouses are usually found attached to barns (and often, these days, are converted into accommodation).

The Coming of the Railway

The London and South Western Railway reached North Tawton in 1865. Plans for a branch line to Bude were dropped, and the railway was extended to Okehampton in 1867, Lydford in 1874, then on to Plymouth, creating a route round the northern and western rim of Dartmoor. The railway boosted the town's fortunes: cloth from the woollen factory, established in the 18th century and a major employer until 1930, was transported out by train; coal to work the mill machinery and for domestic use was brought in; cattle and sheep went to and from Exeter's market, and children to grammar schools in Crediton and Okehampton. Regular passenger services stopped in 1972, but freight is still carried to and from the quarries at Meldon, 3 miles (4.8km) west of Okehampton. The line links with the Tarka Line (the former Exeter and Crediton Railway, see Walk 12) at Crediton. The Dartmoor Railway, operating from Okehampton, also runs seasonal passenger services along part of the line.

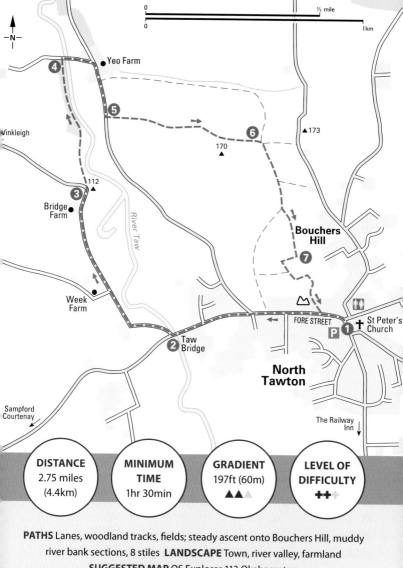

WALK 22 DIRECTIONS

❶ The walk starts from the Jubilee clock tower (1887) in The Square. With your back to the Town Hall bear right down Fore Street signed 'Winkleigh'. Pass No 23; cloth was produced here before moving to the larger mill on the River Taw. Follow the lane out of town to cross 15th-century Taw Bridge.

❷ Turn right on a quiet lane (Tarka Trail). Pass Week Farm and later Bridge Farm.

❸ Soon after, where the lane bears left, bear right on a footpath. Just before a big oak bear left through a kissing gate. Follow the riverside path (muddy in places), carpeted with bluebells in May. Eventually pass a line of lime trees and go through a big gate on to a track.

❹ Turn right to cross the river over single-arched Yeo Bridge and through a gate into a field. Bear right past a barn and along a hedged track to a gate on to an unmetalled road opposite Cider Cottage. Turn right, soon passing the entrance to Yeo Farm, and along a lane.

❺ About 100yds (91m) later turn left over a stile and climb steadily up a narrow hedged path. Cross a stile; turn left up the left edge of a huge field, still climbing; soon enjoy fantastic views over Dartmoor. At the top bear right to cross a double stile in the hedge. Cross the next field, aiming for a stile.

❻ Do not cross the stile, but turn right along the field-edge. Bear left through an open gateway (footpath arrow) and head diagonally across the field, dropping downhill. Pass through a five-bar gate in the hedge; turn right downhill, keeping along the right edge. Cross a double stile to reach a footpath junction; keep ahead on a narrow hedged and banked path under holly trees. Cross a double stile at a field link. The path eventually kinks right then left.

❼ At the next right kink turn left through a kissing gate, then right down the edge of the field, with views over North Tawton ahead. At the bottom turn left to find a kissing gate in the corner, and turn right on a narrow path that drops steeply through allotments, soon passing through a small gate. Meet a track between houses to emerge onto Fore Street. Turn left towards The Square.

🍴 EATING AND DRINKING

North Tawton has the Fountain Inn on Exeter Street, and The Copper Key on Fore Street. Train lovers should head for The Railway Inn, a mile (1.6km) south of town, a traditional warm, welcoming rural pub, with excellent food and walls covered with railway memorabilia. The Bay Tree Delicatessen and Café on The Square has a good takeaway menu and local ice cream.

THE SPECTACULAR HEDDON VALLEY

Discover hanging oakwoods, rushing rivers,
and some of the highest coastal hills in England.

Within the Exmoor National Park, yet still in Devon, the deeply wooded
Heddon Valley, leading to the stark cleft in the coastline at Heddon's Mouth, is
a spectacular sight. There is no obvious main route into the valley, which you
reach by turning off the A39 between Blackmoor Gate and Lynton, and then
winding your way down miles of narrow lanes. Although only one third of
the Exmoor National Park is in Devon, around two-thirds of the National Park
coastline lies within the county, and the stretch seen on this walk is the most
awe-inspiring section.

The National Trust and the West Exmoor Coast
The National Trust owns 2,000 acres (810ha) of land here, much of which is a
Site of Special Scientific Interest. The extensive oak woodlands, deep combes,
coastal heath and some of the highest cliffs in England combine to produce
one of the most magnificent landscape areas in Devon. The land immediately
to the west and east of Heddon's Mouth Cleave rises very steeply up scree-
covered slopes to a staggering 820ft (250m), and Great Hangman, the highest
coastal hill in southern England at over 1,000ft (305m) lies just beyond
Holdstone Down to the west. Exmoor, unlike Dartmoor, runs right up to the
coast, and the cliff scenery towards Combe Martin on this walk is superb.
There's no access to the sea between Heddon's Mouth and Combe Martin,
5 miles (8km) to the west. The National Trust information centre in the
Heddon Valley is open from two weeks before Easter to the end of October.

Lynton Rocks
If you have time, have a look at another extraordinary piece of coastal
landscape in the area: the Valley of Rocks, just west of Lynton. This craggy, dry
valley is different from anywhere else on Exmoor, and is characterised by its
jagged sandstone tors, formed through weathering over thousands of years.
There is a pleasant and easy walk east into Lynton along the North Walk coast
path from here. Look out for the feral goats that live on the rocky slopes,
which were reintroduced here in the 19th century.

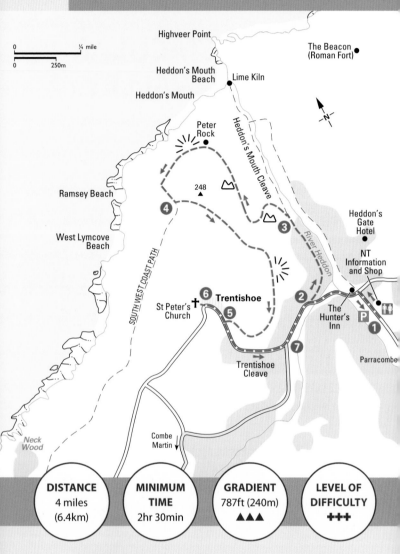

Highveer Point

The Beacon (Roman Fort)

Heddon's Mouth Beach

Lime Kiln

Heddon's Mouth

Peter Rock

Heddon's Mouth Cleave

Ramsey Beach

248

Heddon's Gate Hotel

West Lymcove Beach

NT Information and Shop

4

SOUTH WEST COAST PATH

3

River Heddon

2

St Peter's Church

6 Trentishoe

5

The Hunter's Inn

1

P

7

Parracombe

Trentishoe Cleave

Neck Wood

Combe Martin

0 — ¼ mile
0 — 250m

N

DISTANCE	MINIMUM TIME	GRADIENT	LEVEL OF DIFFICULTY
4 miles (6.4km)	2hr 30min	787ft (240m) ▲▲▲	+++

PATHS Wooded tracks, exposed coast path and quiet lanes
LANDSCAPE Deep, wooded river valleys and very high cliffs
SUGGESTED MAP OS Explorer OL9 Exmoor **START/FINISH** Grid reference:
SS 655481 **DOG FRIENDLINESS** Dogs to be kept under control at all times; on
lead on coast path where sheep often graze **PARKING** National Trust car park at
Heddon's Gate (honesty box) **PUBLIC TOILETS** Opposite car park
NOTE Not recommended for those who suffer from vertigo

WALK 23 DIRECTIONS

❶ Walk towards The Hunter's Inn, bearing left on Josey's Lane to pass the building. Cross the River Heddon, then the Blackmoor Water (look out for Harry's Orchard to the right, open to the public).

❷ Turn right through a gate signed 'Access to Coast Path and Heddon's Mouth' and keep along a woodland track until a Coast Path sign to Combe Martin directs you left, uphill.

🅗 EATING AND DRINKING

The Hunters Inn, built in 1904 on the site of the original thatched inn, which was destroyed by fire in 1895, is a free house, with accommodation. The Fox and Goose Inn at Parracombe, to the south, is an interesting building, with good food.

---

❸ A steep zig-zag climb is rewarded with amazing views across the valley and inland. Keep going along the narrow path, which runs parallel to the valley to reach the coast above Heddon's Mouth, then turns left towards Peter Rock. The cliffs here are over 650ft (198m) high and sheer, and the path is narrow and exposed – take care. Continue along the path, which runs inland to meet a wall.

❹ Turn left, signed 'Trentishoe Church'. This lovely level, grassy path runs inland 720ft (220m) above the valley of the River Heddon, and the views over the deep combes that join the main valley are glorious. It's a very easy walk, and a welcome relief from the Coast Path.

❺ The path meets a lane; for a look at St Peter's Church turn right uphill for 200yds (183m). It's hard to work out why there should be a church here – it's in the middle of nowhere – but 96 people are recorded as living here in 1891. The church is mentioned in the Episcopal Register of 1260. The tiny castellated tower dates from the 15th century, as do parts of the west wall, and the north and south walls of the nave; and there's a wonderful musicians' gallery, built in 1771.

❻ From the church walk down Trentishoe Hill (unsuitable for vehicles) through wooded Trentishoe Cleave.

❼ Bear left at the valley bottom by two cottages. Follow the lane past a footpath sign to Heddon's Mouth, cross the Blackmoor and Heddon rivers to The Hunters Inn. Bear right to your car.

🐾 ON THE WALK

Exmoor ponies – the closest native breed to a truly wild equine – have been used on these coastal hills (and elsewhere on Exmoor) to encourage regeneration of the heather moorland. Visit the Moorland Mousie Trust near Dulverton to find out more.

BURGH ISLAND PARADISE

A glimpse of 1930s celebrity lifestyle on a South Devon island – and have a drink at one of Devon's oldest inns.

The broad, sandy beaches and dunes at Bigbury-on-Sea and Bantham, at the mouth of the River Avon south-west of Kingsbridge, attract holidaymakers every summer, drawn by the appeal of sun, sand and sea. There's no doubt that this is a perfect spot for a family day out. Gone are the days of the 16th or 17th centuries when Bigbury was merely famous for its catches of pilchards. But there's something else appealing about this part of the South Devon coast. Just off Bigbury beach, 307yds (282m) from shore, lies craggy Burgh Island, with its famous hotel gazing at the mainland. This extraordinary island is completely surrounded by the sea at high tide but is accessible via the weird and wonderful sea tractor that ploughs its way through the waters.

The Enigma of Burgh Island

The island was known as la Burgh in the 15th century, and later Borough Island. There was a chapel dedicated to St Michael on its summit in 1411, and it has been likened to the much larger St Michael's Mount in Cornwall. The remains of a 'huer's hut' at the top of the island – a fisherman's lookout – is evidence of the times when pilchard fishing was a mainstay of life here too, hence the building of the Pilchard Inn, housed in one of the original fisherman's cottages. But it is the island's more recent history that is so fascinating. It was bought in 1929 by wealthy industrialist Archibald Nettlefold, who built the Burgh Island Hotel, much as we see it today. He ran it as a guest house for friends and celebrities, and it became a highly fashionable venue in the 1930s. Noël Coward was among the visitors and it is thought that Edward, Prince of Wales and Wallis Simpson escaped from the limelight here; but the island's most famous connection has to be with Agatha Christie. Two of her books – *Evil Under the Sun* and *And Then There Were None* – were written here, and the influence of the hotel and its location on her writing is clear. By the mid 1980s the hotel had fallen into disrepair, and two London fashion consultants, Beatrice and Tony Porter, bought the island and restored the hotel to its original art deco glory, complete with the famous Palm Court and authentic Twenties cocktail bar.

Opposite: Burgh Island

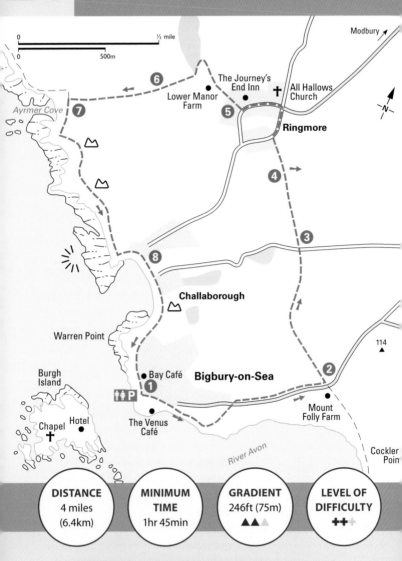

DISTANCE	MINIMUM TIME	GRADIENT	LEVEL OF DIFFICULTY
4 miles (6.4km)	1hr 45min	246ft (75m) ▲▲△	✚✚✚

PATHS Fields, tracks (muddy in winter) and coast path, 3 stiles
LANDSCAPE Rolling coastal farmland and cliff top
SUGGESTED MAP OS Explorer OL20 South Devon
START/FINISH Grid reference: SX 652442
DOG FRIENDLINESS Keep under control at all times; on lead through fields
PARKING Huge car park at Bigbury-on-Sea
PUBLIC TOILETS At car park; also in car park at Bantham

WALK 24 DIRECTIONS

❶ Leave the car park through the entrance. Follow 'Coast Path' signs right, thenalong a short stretch of low-lying clifftop. Turn left before bungalows, then left to the road. Cross over, go through a kissing gate and turn right uphill, passing through two big gates, to reach a path junction near Mount Folly Farm.

❷ Turn left along a gritty track (signed 'Ringmore'). At the field top is a path junction; go through the kissing gate and keep ahead downhill, signed 'Ringmore', with a fence right. Pass through a metal gate, drop through a kissing gate, keep ahead to another on a farm track; walk up the next field, crossing a stile on to a lane.

> ⓦ **EATING AND DRINKING**
> The Bay Café at Bigbury has great views over Burgh Island, as does The Venus Café. The atmospheric Journey's End Inn is one of Devon's oldest inns; the original building was constructed in 1180, and the inn dates from the 13th century. It was once used as a Royalist meeting place. There are plenty of refreshments at Challaborough, too.

❸ Cross over, following signs for Ringmore, through a metal gate. Walk down into the next combe, keeping the hedgebank right. Cross the stream at the bottom on a concrete walkway, and over a stile. Ignore the path left, but go straight ahead, uphill, through

a plantation and gate on to a narrow path between a fence and hedge.

❹ Pass through a kissing gate, bear right then turn immediately left uphill to a path junction; pass through the kissing gate and follow the path to Ringmore. Turn right at the lane, then left at the church to find The Journey's End Inn on the right.

❺ From the pub turn right down the narrow lane which gives way to a footpath. It winds round gardens to meet a tarmac lane. Turn left downhill. Walk straight on down the track, eventually passing Lower Manor Farm, and keep going down past the 'National Trust Ayrmer Cove' notice. After a small gate and stream crossing keep straight on at a path junction.

❻ Pass through a kissing gate and walk towards the cove on a grassy path above the combe (left). Pass through gates and over a stile to gain the beach.

❼ Follow coast path signs ('Challaborough') left over a small footbridge then climb very steeply uphill to the cliff top. The cliffs are unstable here – take care. The path leads to Challaborough, a holiday park.

❽ Turn right along the beach road and pick up the track uphill along the coast towards Bigbury-on-Sea. Go straight on to meet the tarmac road, then bear right on the coast path to the car park.

BELSTONE CLEAVE AND COSDON HILL

Along the rocky valley of the young River Taw,
with a return across the wide-open spaces of Cosdon Hill.

The pretty little village of Belstone – an attractive mix of cob and thatch
cottages and granite-built Victorian houses – sits 1,000ft (305m) up on the
northern edge of Dartmoor. Much of the parish is open moorland, within
which can be found a number of granite tors and archaeological monuments.

On the slopes of Belstone Common, the Nine Maidens stone circle dates
from Bronze Age times, though legend has it that it represents a group of
maidens turned to stone for dancing on the Sabbath.

River Taw

The infant Taw is particularly lovely as it rushes through rocky Belstone
Cleave. The Henry Williamson bridge, passed on Point ❹, is inscribed with
words taken from *Tarka the Otter* (see Walk 37) which sum up the character of
the river at this point: 'Amid rocks and scree that in falling had smashed the
trunks and torn out the roots of willow, thorns and hollies…It wandered away
from the moor, a proper river with bridges, brooks, islands and mills.'

On the return stretch look for a rough granite wall that crosses the ridge
south of Belstone Tor. Known as the Irishman's Wall, various stories justify its
construction. The most plausible is that it was built in the early 19th century
– by Irish workers. The men of Belstone and Okehampton, however, were
having none of it, and toppled parts of the wall over, rendering it useless.

The Finch Foundry

A short extension to the walk from Point ❺ will take you to the Finch Foundry,
now in the hands of the National Trust. A working foundry from 1814 to 1960,
around 400 tools for agricultural and mining purposes were produced daily
at the foundry during its heyday. There was a grinding house on the site in
the 13th century, powered by water leated from the Taw – you can see a sluice
gate and leat at Cleave Mill on the opposite bank during Point ❹ of the walk
– and in the 19th century a smithy was set up by the Finch family. Apart from
tools the site also produced serge for army uniforms, made from local wool.
There are daily working demonstrations when the foundry is open.

Opposite: The River Taw on Taw Marsh near Belstone

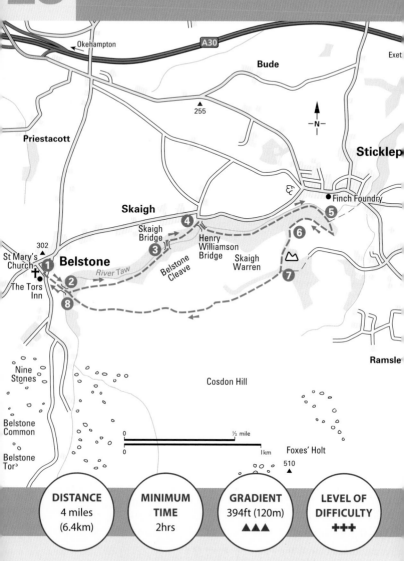

DISTANCE	MINIMUM TIME	GRADIENT	LEVEL OF DIFFICULTY
4 miles (6.4km)	2hrs	394ft (120m) ▲▲▲	+++

PATHS Riverside path rough underfoot with rocks and roots, steep ascent to
Cosdon Hill **LANDSCAPE** River valley and open moorland
SUGGESTED MAP OS Explorer OL28 Dartmoor
START/FINISH Grid reference: SX 620935 **DOG FRIENDLINESS** Under control at
all times, on lead in nesting season (1 March–15 July) **PARKING** Laneside or car
park in Belstone (free) **PUBLIC TOILETS** None on route, nearest at Okehampton
NOTE Do not attempt this walk in misty or inclement weather

WALK 25 DIRECTIONS

❶ The walk starts from The Tors Inn. Pass the pub and on reaching the Great Green bear left off the lane across the grass, dropping to soon pick up a track that descends to the River Taw. Bear right to cross it on a footbridge.

❷ Turn left past the ford, then right away from the river, with a wall left. After 100yds (91m) bear left on a narrower path that ascends through gorse; after a few paces, where a wall comes into view ahead right, bear slightly left downhill. The path runs along bracken-covered slopes, eventually dropping steeply, then follows the riverbank (very rough in places). Pass craggy Ivy Tor.

❸ Reach a path junction at Skaigh Bridge. Turn left across the river, signed Skaigh, and climb to a T-junction; turn right along a woodland path.

❹ At the next path junction turn right (signed Sticklepath) and pick your way through trees, bearing left towards the river and the Henry Williamson bridge.

🍴 EATING AND DRINKING

The Tors Inn is a friendly and down-to-earth place to go for a refreshing drink or bite to eat after tramping across the moor. Cream teas are served in Belstone Village Hall, opposite the village car park, on summer Sunday afternoons, and there's a café at the Finch Foundry.

Cross over and continue along the rocky riverside path to pass a weir (left); continue on more even ground and through a small gate. Cottages come into view on the opposite bank.

❺ Reach a footpath junction. (To visit the Finch Foundry turn left here.) On the main walk, turn right on a public bridlepath to the moor (also Tarka Trail and Taw–Teign Link) and ascend steeply, soon turning sharp right and climbing through Skaigh Wood. The path levels a little, broadens under oaks, and passes through a gate.

❻ Follow the bridlepath left and climb under beeches, with a wall left. Follow the wall uphill. Eventually go through a gate on the edge of Cosdon Hill.

❼ Turn right on a grassy track, keeping ahead where the wall ends. After 100yds (91m) look left uphill to see a tall Belstone/South Tawton boundary stone; keep ahead to join a broad grassy path that descends from that stone, and continue gently downhill. The path crosses the Ivy Tor Water and eventually starts to descend, aiming towards the church tower. Meet a walled enclosure; follow the wall downhill. At the bottom edge bear left on a grassy and rock-slab path that leads to the footbridge.

❽ Cross the River Taw and retrace your steps up the track, bearing left to cross the lane and return to The Tors.

CROCKERN TOR AND WISTMAN'S WOOD

Enjoy a wealth of Dartmoor history and legend on this lovely route above the valley of the East Dart river.

One of Dartmoor's most visited natural attractions, Wistman's Wood (National Nature Reserve) is one of only three remaining patches of ancient high-altitude oak woodland, which would in prehistoric times have covered the moor. The others – Blackator Copse near Meldon Reservoir, and Piles Copse in the Erme Valley north of Ivybridge – are far less accessible, hence the popularity of Wistman's Wood.

Myths and Legends

It is a magical spot: a dense mass of stunted oak trees, festooned with mosses and lichens, growing amongst a clutter of mossy granite boulders. Not surprisingly the Devil is linked with this atmospheric spot. It is said to be home to his terrifying Wisht hounds, who drive sinners across the treacherous boulders until they fall and are seized upon by the bloodthirsty creatures. Longaford Tor too enjoys its share of legends, said to be home to the Ghost Foxes of Dartmoor. The remains of a missing shepherd were once found there, and every year during the week before Christmas the foxes' haunted cries may be heard around the tor.

The Stannary Parliament

Point ❸ leads to Crockern Tor, site of Dartmoor's stannary parliament, sited at a central point on the moor between the four stannary towns. The first stannary charter was granted in 1201 in the reign of King John I; under Edward I stannary towns (to administer the tin-mining industry) were established round the edge of the moor (Ashburton, Chagford and Tavistock in 1305, later joined by Plympton). The charter set up stannary courts, which administered a set of laws to regulate the industry. The earliest known sitting of the stannary parliament at Crockern was in 1494. By the mid-1700s the tin industry had started to decline; the last stannary parliament at Crockern took place in 1749, and the stannary courts were abolished in 1896. At Crockern Tor you can still see Parliament Rock, a large natural amphitheatre, and rock-hewn tables and seats.

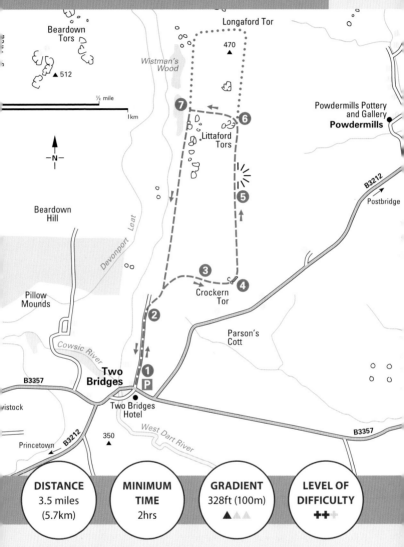

Beardown
Tors

▲ 512

½ mile

1 km

—N—

Beardown
Hill

Pillow
Mounds

Cowsic River

B3357

Two
Bridges

vistock

Princetown

B3212

350
▲

Longaford Tor

470
▲

Wistman's
Wood

7

6

Littaford
Tors

Powdermills Pottery
and Gallery
Powdermills

B3212

Postbridge

Devonport Leat

5

3

4

Crockern
Tor

2

1
P

Two Bridges
Hotel

West Dart River

Parson's
Cott

B3357

DISTANCE	MINIMUM TIME	GRADIENT	LEVEL OF DIFFICULTY
3.5 miles (5.7km)	2hrs	328ft (100m) ▲▲▲	++✛

PATHS Pathless moorland, rough underfoot and wet in places after rainfall,
1 stile **LANDSCAPE** Moorland **SUGGESTED MAP** OS Explorer OL28 Dartmoor
START/FINISH Grid reference: SX 609750
DOG FRIENDLINESS Under control at all times; on lead in nesting season
(1 March–15 July) **PARKING** Quarry car park opposite Two Bridges Hotel (free)
PUBLIC TOILETS None on route, nearest at Princetown
NOTE Do not attempt this walk in misty weather

WALK 26 DIRECTIONS

❶ From the car park opposite The Two Bridges Hotel. Pass through the gate heading away from the road, and follow the track, with the West Dart river across marshy ground below right.

❷ Follow the rocky path along the wall to the right of Crockern Cottage to meet a footpath post; keep ahead uphill as signed on a rough track through gorse bushes. Look upvalley for the first signs of the stunted oaks of Wistman's Wood clinging to the eastern slopes of the valley, with pyramidal Longaford Tor above. Stay on the track, which heads towards a gap in the wall ahead.

❸ Before reaching that bear right to pass through another gap, aiming for Crockern Tor on the hilltop ahead. Cross pathless and rocky moorland to reach the tor, site of the old stannary parliament, with wonderful views south.

❹ From the tor turn left and then head north along the ridge, parallel to the West Dart valley, aiming for the Littaford Tors, with pointy Longaford Tor beyond. Look across the valley to the Beardown Tors on the edge of the military ranges. Note also the Devonport Leat (built in 1790 to carry water to Devonport Dockyard in Plymouth) running along the contours on the west side of the valley.

A wall comes in right; pass over a stile in the wall corner ahead.

❺ Continue to the northernmost outcrop of the Littaford Tors; look right towards Powdermills, site of an old gunpowder factory. Pass to the right for a view of the rocks. (To extend the walk keep ahead to Longaford, then turn left into the valley to Wistman's Wood.)

❻ Bear left and pick your way round the tor, soon bearing right to walk downhill towards Wistman's Wood (note there is no obvious path and the way is studded with granite blocks).

❼ On reaching a rough path about 50yds (46m) from the wood turn left. The path soon forks; take the right fork, which drops towards the wood. Keep ahead, leaving the wood behind, with the river below right, to cross a stile in a wall. Follow the path back to pass through a wall gap, then past Crockern Cottage to return to your car.

> **⑪ EATING AND DRINKING**
>
> The Two Bridges Hotel opposite the parking area is a traditional country hotel, with roaring log fires in winter and comfortable sofas to sink into. At Powdermills Pottery and Gallery – where the work of local craftspeople is on sale – a mile (1.6km) to the north-east towards Postbridge, cream teas are served in the summer months.

Opposite: Crockern Tor near Two Bridges

ARLINGTON COURT AND DEERPARK WOOD

An up-and-down walk through the lovely beechwoods and riverside paths of the Wider Estate.

The National Trust's Arlington Court estate in North Devon comprises 2,700 acres (1,094ha) of rolling green fields and thickly wooded valleys around the Yeo River and its tributaries. This particularly peaceful spot lies well off the beaten track, and is a delight for the walkers. Not only is there a good network of public rights of way threading the Wider Estate, but the National Trust has also opened up several additional routes here, giving a number of options for walks through a most attractive landscape. The presence of good quantities of oak and beech trees produces wonderful colours in autumn.

The Chichester Family

The Arlington Court estate was owned by the Chichester family from 1384, and given to the National Trust by Rosalie Chichester – born in 1865, and the last of the family to reside there – two years before her death in 1949. The present rather severe neoclassical house was built in 1822 for Colonel John Chichester (the foundations of a 16th-century dwelling can be found to the south of the house).

The house seen today was designed by a local architect Thomas Lee, who also designed the Wellington Monument in Somerset. In the 1860s, under Sir Bruce Chichester, a new wing was added, and the rather grand stableyard, now housing the Carriage Museum, constructed. The house still has the intimate atmosphere of a family home and is full of treasures collected by Miss Chichester on her world travels. As the only child of the flamboyant Sir Bruce Chichester she had an adventurous childhood, and in her early years sailed on two world cruises aboard her father's schooner *Erminia*.

Look out for horse-drawn vehicles as you enter the estate. The National Trust Carriage Museum is housed in the old stableyard, comprising examples over 40 vehicles that might have been found at any substantial country house in the 19th century, from a two-wheeled child's carriage and coffin carrier to a fine original state chariot.

—N—

115 ▲

River Yeo

A39

P 1

2

Arlington

Bratton Fleming

Old Kitchen Tearoom
Arlington Court

St James Church ✝

3

National Carriage Museum

8

4

Cairn

Barton Court

Woolley Wood

Smallacombe Bridge

7

Wider Estate

Tucker's Bridge

5

Deerpark Wood

6

240 ▲

Barnstaple

½ mile

1km

Loxhore ✝

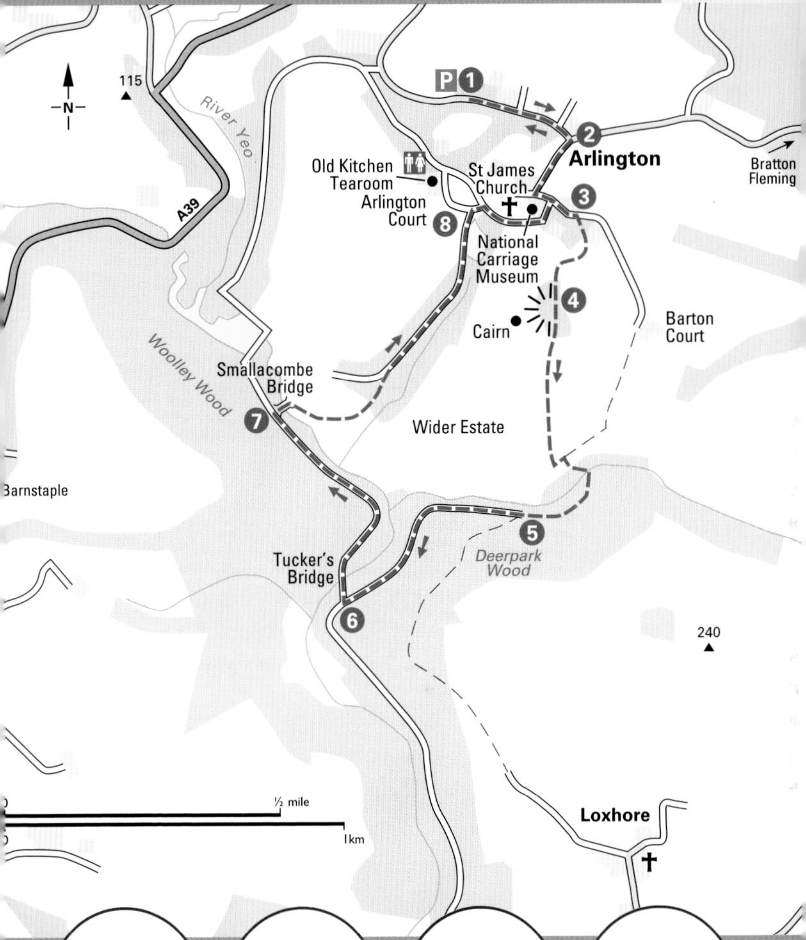

DISTANCE	MINIMUM TIME	GRADIENT	LEVEL OF DIFFICULTY
3 miles (4.8km)	1hr 30min	230ft (70m) ▲▲△	✚✚✚

PATHS Field tracks and woodland paths; some muddy after wet weather
LANDSCAPE Rolling parkland and wooded river valley
SUGGESTED MAP OS Explorer OL9 Exmoor
START/FINISH Grid reference: SS 611408
DOG FRIENDLINESS On lead through parkland **PARKING** Car park at Arlington Court (free) **PUBLIC TOILETS** At Arlington Court **NOTE** The National Trust Estate is open to walkers all year round from dawn to dusk

WALK 27 DIRECTIONS

1 From the car park – with views north to Exmoor's coastal hills – turn left along the lane (opposite the pedestrian entrance to the house and gardens) to pass estate cottages.

2 Where the lane bears sharp left, turn right down a dead-end lane. The lane bears left and reduces to a track to meet a junction of paths, with Arlington Court signed right; keep ahead to pass the old sawmill (left).

3 At the next path junction turn right on a blue-waymarked bridlepath through a strip of woodland signed to Deerpark Wood. Pass through a gate into a field and turn right. At the field end turn left through a wooden gate, and keep uphill into woodland.

4 Pass a viewpoint, right. Pass through two gates; continue downhill. Pass through a clump of woodland and two open gateways, and along the right edge of the next field (fenced). The path bears left through a gate into woodland, drops steadily to cross a stream, and rises to a junction.

5 Bear right downhill, signed 'Loxhore Cottage via Tucker's Bridge', following a green arrow. At the next junction (Loxhore church is signed left) keep ahead along the broad path that passes beneath beech trees, initially with a stream below right, eventually dropping gently to meet a track.

6 Turn right to cross Tucker's Bridge over the Yeo River, which flows into the Taw at Barnstaple. Follow the track as it bears left under beech trees, with the pretty Yeo River right, to meet a path junction; the lake and bird hide are signed ahead.

7 Turn right to cross Smallacombe Bridge and go through a gate into parkland. Follow the grassy path as it bears right and ascends gently to pass three huge lime trees clumped together, and through a gate into woodland. Follow the track uphill, passing a junction, eventually to reach the edge of the gardens at Arlington Court. Pass a pond with waterlilies, right, to meet a gravel path.

> **🍴 EATING AND DRINKING**
> Arlington Court sits in remote countryside off Exmoor's western edge. The nearest pub is The White Hart in Bratton Fleming. The Old Kitchen Tearoom at the house serves light lunches and teas; jams and preserves made with produce from the kitchen garden are on sale in the shop.

8 Turn left for refreshments, main house and gardens (note there is an entrance charge); otherwise turn right, soon bearing right again to pass St James Church, the stableyard and the Carriage Museum. Bear left to the sawmill path junction; turn left and retrace your steps to the car park.

DRIZZLECOMBE AND THE GIANT'S BASIN

A walk of big skies and far-reaching views to one of Dartmoor's most impressive prehistoric sites.

Within minutes of starting the walk you'll be rewarded with expansive views of some of the widest landscapes Dartmoor has to offer. The focus of the route is Drizzlecombe (also known as 'Thrushelcombe'; the old moorland name for a thrush was 'drishel'), a broad sweep of sloping moorland above the banks of the infant River Plym, renowned for its wealth of prehistoric monuments. The moor's tallest standing stone (menhir) at 15ft (4.5m) – the Drizzlecombe Longstone – is passed on Point ❺. And as far as navigation goes this triangular route (largely along rough tracks) is easy to follow, despite passing through a very remote landscape.

A Long History of Occupation

The Drizzlecombe Valley is an important archaeological site for its wealth of Bronze Age monuments including the impressive Giant's Cairn. The extensive array includes three stone rows, standing stones, cists, cairns, pounds and hut circles, and evidence of a settlement 4,000 years ago at Whittenknowles Rocks.

You may come across Highland cattle grazing in the area, you will certainly see tough little black Galloways, one of the oldest and purest breeds in the country. These hardy beasts do well on the poorest of land and are renowned as a traditional hill farm breed. Belted Galloways have a broad white band around the body.

Ditsworthy Warren House

Remotely situated Ditsworthy Warren House, reached on Point ❻, dates from the 16th century. Once known as Ware's Warren after the family who lived there, Ditsworthy Warren was at one time the largest commercial rabbit warren on Dartmoor, covering almost 1,100 acres (445ha) and rearing rabbits for food and skins. Although the practice was banned in the 1950s, at one time the greatest concentration of warrens was found in this part of the moor. Rabbits would be taken to the warren house to be skinned and cleaned; it is recorded that at Ditsworthy large kills were carried on a donkey.

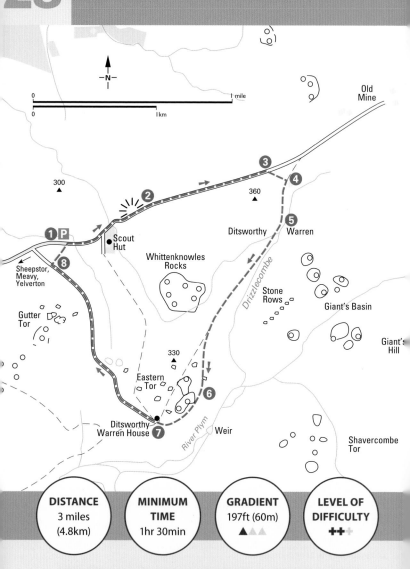

DISTANCE	MINIMUM TIME	GRADIENT	LEVEL OF DIFFICULTY
3 miles (4.8km)	1hr 30min	197ft (60m) ▲▲▲	++

PATHS Rough tracks and grassy moorland paths, often wet underfoot
LANDSCAPE Moorland **SUGGESTED MAP** OS Explorer OL9 Dartmoor
START/FINISH Grid reference: SX 579673
DOG FRIENDLINESS Under control at all times; on lead in nesting season
(1 March–15 July) **PARKING** Parking area near Gutter Tor Scout Hut
PUBLIC TOILETS None on route **NOTE** Do not attempt in misty weather; much
of the route is very wet after heavy rainfall

WALK 28 DIRECTIONS

❶ Start from a rough parking area just above the ford of the Sheepstor Brook near the old Scout Hut at Gutter Tor. Cross the bridge over the stream and follow the rough track to the left of the Scout Hut into broad, sweeping moorland, ascending gently. Look left to see huge blocky Sheeps Tor, and pointed Leather Tor to its right, both rising above Burrator Reservoir.

❷ Follow the broad track, rocky underfoot, which eventually leads to Eylesbarrow Tin Mine. Before reaching the mine the track levels, with views to Shavercombe and Legis Tors on the south side of the Plym Valley.

❸ Just past a boundary stone (1917) bear right on another track that descends gently to meet a crossroads of rough tracks, with the rounded corner of a moss-covered dilapidated wall on the opposite left corner.

❹ Turn right and walk along the edge of Drizzlecombe (boggy ground below left), soon passing the remains of old buildings, with sweeping views ahead across Ditsworthy Warren. Where a vague track bears left across the combe keep straight on.

❺ Soon cross a leat; continue on a broad grassy path that runs ahead through bracken, with Drizzlecombe below left. Our forward route runs to the left of Eastern Tor ahead. Look left to see the Drizzlecombe Longstone, with another standing stone to its right, and another ahead to the right of the path. Cross a narrow path and keep ahead, soon bearing slightly left with the grassy path towards the Plym, passing a recumbent gatepost on route.

❻ Meet a cart track that runs left towards the stone rows and turn right. Follow the rutted track parallel to the River Plym. Scrubby conifers and dilapidated walls appear ahead, marking the site of Ditsworthy Warren House overlooking the Plym Valley.

❼ Pass the house, and cross a small stream to meet a broad and muddy track. Bear right along it; craggy Gutter Tor soon comes into view ahead, and later the conifers around the Scout Hut, right.

❽ Pass round a gate; a few paces later bear right across rough grassland to meet the approach lane to the parking area and turn right to your car.

🍴 EATING AND DRINKING

The Royal Oak Inn at Meavy dates from the 15th century when it was a church house. The Rock Inn at Yelverton, originally a coaching inn, has been in the same family for more than 120 years. In the late 1880s it was run as the Blatchford Hotel by two maiden aunts, and at one time had its own cattle, hens, pigs and a huge vegetable garden.

THE PLYMOUTH AND DARTMOOR RAILWAY

Walk along the route of Devon's first 'iron railroad' through the heart of the Princetown quarries.

This wonderful – and relatively untaxing – moorland walk is packed with interest from the very start. Not only is Dartmoor's highest town, Princetown – and its notorious prison – just up the road, there are also disused granite quarries, the former line of the old Plymouth and Dartmoor Railway, and some of the best Bronze Age structures on the moor a stone's throw from the route.

The walk is also blessed with sweeping views in every direction, from the majestic heights of Great Staple and Great Mis tors to the north and as far south as Plymouth Sound. Note that there is one stream crossing, and no bridge; it's a case of hopping from one bank to the other or, at times of low water, wading across the ford.

Tyrwhitt's Railroad

The Plymouth and Dartmoor Railway was the brainchild of Thomas Tyrwhitt, a friend of the Prince Regent (later George IV), who in 1796 was appointed as auditor to the Duchy of Cornwall. He determined to build a flourishing settlement on the high moor – Princetown – though many of his schemes were unsuccessful. To this end he developed the local quarries, and laid the foundation stone for the new prison in March 1806.

In 1823 he built the horse-drawn Plymouth and Dartmoor Railroad (eventually extended into Princetown village) to take granite out of the quarries at Foggintor, Swelltor and King's Tor. The line was taken over by the Great Western Railway in 1883, and closed in 1956. Today it makes for an excellent walking and off-road cycling route.

Merrival Monuments

North of King's Tor – accessed from Point ❽ on the walk – lies the Merrivale ceremonial complex of late-neolithic/early Bronze Age monuments, one of the most significant on the moor, comprising a double and a single stone row, standing stones, burial cairns and a stone circle, as well as a later Bronze Age settlement. The stone rows were once believed to be the work of druids.

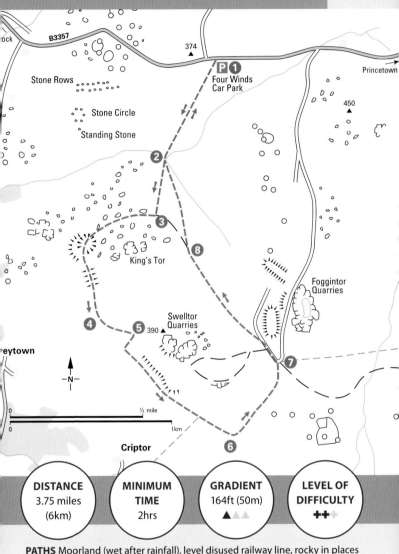

DISTANCE	MINIMUM TIME	GRADIENT	LEVEL OF DIFFICULTY
3.75 miles (6km)	2hrs	164ft (50m) ▲▲▲	++

PATHS Moorland (wet after rainfall), level disused railway line, rocky in places

LANDSCAPE Moorland **SUGGESTED MAP** OS Explorer OL28 Dartmoor

START/FINISH Grid reference: SX 561749

DOG FRIENDLINESS Under control at all times; on lead in nesting season
(1 March–15 July) **PARKING** Four Winds car park (free)

PUBLIC TOILETS None on route; nearest in Princetown car park,
3 miles/4.8km south-east **NOTE** Do not attempt this walk in misty weather;
one stream crossing (no bridge)

WALK 29 DIRECTIONS

1 With your back to the road walk through a narrow gap in the wall and past a solitary conifer. Pass through a gap in the next wall, and cross the leat (supplying local farms and cottages) on a granite slab bridge. Bear slightly right, downhill, to pass a boundary stone (marked 'T and A' for Tavistock and Ashburton), aiming for the bottom corner of a wall that runs downhill beyond the stream. Pass through a bank to meet the streambank.

🍴 EATING AND DRINKING

The Fox Tor Café in Princetown is the perfect place to go after a moorland walk, especially if you're damp. It's warm and welcoming, serves good food and drink, with no objections to wet coats and muddy boots. The Plume of Feathers, the town's oldest building (1785) has slate floors, low beams, open fires, a camping field and bunkhouse.

---

2 Bear left to wade through the ford, or right towards the wall corner on the opposite bank to cross at a shallower, rocky, spot. Follow the wall uphill; where it curves right keep ahead up a grassy path, weaving through granite blocks, to the disued railway track.

3 Turn right along the embanked track, with views west to Bodmin Moor. Nearer at hand can be seen the rugged outline of Vixen Tor, which has the greatest drop of Dartmoor's tors (100ft/30.5m). The line curves left through a cutting, with views to Plymouth Sound, and across the wooded valley of the River Walkham right, and crosses a bridge.

4 Soon after, at an obvious junction of tracks, bear left on a grassy track, a siding running into the quarry at King's Tor. After about 250yds (229m), note 12 granite corbels; made for London Bridge but surplus to requirements.

5 From the corbels bear right to the main track, and turn left past ruins and spoil heaps of Swelltor Quarries, soon passing a bridleway, right; note the line of the railway running away ahead.

6 About 200yds (183m) later, as the line bears right, and opposite a gate on the right, turn left up a rough path, along a broken-down granite wall. Where the wall bears away right follow the path, bearing left uphill to meet the railway line at a path junction.

7 Turn left along the line, soon taking the left fork at a junction; the car park and Great Mis Tor come into view. The track bears left round the hill slope; where the wall originally followed up from the stream comes into view bear right downhill, aiming for the bottom wall corner.

8 Cross the stream, bear slightly right through the bank ahead. Follow the broad grassy path past the boundary stone to the car park.

Opposite: Ramblers at Merrivale

THE MYSTERIES
OF THE DEWERSTONE

Industrial archaeology along the Plym –
and a hard climb past the eerie Dewerstone Crags.

This is a popular walk, not only because of its proximity to Plymouth, but also because of the wealth of obvious industrial archaeological interest. The best way to experience this is to start from Cadover Bridge, on the edge of the open moor towards the Lee Moor China Clay Works. You follow the route of the pipeline that carried the china clay in suspension from the works to the drying kilns at Shaugh Bridge (seen in the car park), via settling tanks, the remains of which are passed on the walk.

A Tale of Two Bridges

The area around Shaugh Bridge is a Site of Special Scientific Interest (SSSI), nationally important for plants and wildlife, and there is a constant conservation programme going on here. The bridge itself dates from the late 1820s, and replaces one that was badly damaged in January 1823. Cadover Bridge was named in a charter of 1291 as 'ponta de Cada worth', so its name probably derives from *cad*, Celtic for 'skirmish'. The Plym is also referred to as Plymma, from the Celtic *pilim*, 'to roll'.

The Devil (locally known as 'Dewer') has long been associated with the Dewerstone. The Devil's fearsome pack of wisht hounds are said to roam the desolate moors at night, seeking unrepentant sinners, whom they drive over the edge of the crags to the Devil waiting below. And the woods near the Dewerstone are said to be haunted at night by a huge, evil dog with red eyes. Such stories are common in moorland areas, and perhaps date back to a time when wolves still inhabited the more remote parts of the country.

Ancient Remains

There are Bronze Age hut circles and cairns on Wigford Down, dating to at least 1000 BC, and Iron Age fortifications protecting the summit of the ridge. Cadover Cross, passed on Point ❽ , is an ancient restored cross set on the line of the Monastic Way between Plympton and Tavistock. It was found lying recumbent in 1873 and re-erected, only to fall and be put up again in 1915, set in a large socket stone. It stands over 7ft 6in (2m) tall.

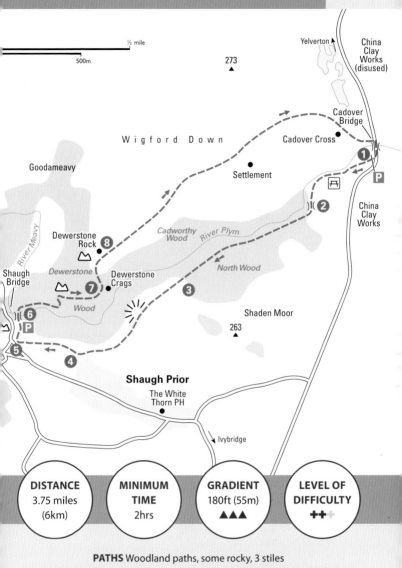

WALK 30 DIRECTIONS

❶ From the car park, walk away from Cadover Bridge, with the river on your right. Pass through a kissing gate and through a small willow plantation.

❷ A wooden ladder down a bank leads to a stile and footbridge into North Wood. Keep ahead on the rocky path which follows the course of a large clay pipe, which appears above ground intermittently.

❸ Leave North Wood over a stile. Follow the path through an open brackeny area; the Plym is below on the right. Note the Dewerstone Crags, popular with climbers, on the other side of the valley. The path leads into silver birch and oak past a settling tank, then forks. Take the right fork downhill to a path junction and gate.

❹ Turn right inside the wire fence, following the footpath sign 'Shaugh Bridge'. Stay within the woods as the yellow-waymarked path twists downhill. The path leads over a stile to pass settling tanks (right), and eventually meets a road.

❺ Turn immediately right and follow the narrow path on and eventually down steps leading into Shaugh Bridge car park. Turn right to walk through the car park towards the river.

❻ Cross the river via the footbridge to enter Goodameavy (National Trust). Follow the path right. It becomes a restored rocky track leading above the river and winds steeply uphill, so take your time. After a sharp left bend take the next path right (narrower but still paved). Continue uphill until you are level with the top of granite buttresses (Dewerstone Crags) on the right.

❼ Bear right and scramble steeply uphill, passing more buttresses (right), eventually to leave the woods and enter moorland to Dewerstone Rock.

❽ Turn 90 degrees right at the rock and follow the right-hand grassy path along the edge of the valley to pass Oxen Tor and over Wigford Down, keeping Cadworthy Wood and the Plym Valley on your right. Keep straight on to the boundary wall of the wood, then follow the wall around fields. Eventually the wall bears right and you walk downhill past Cadover Cross. Bear left at the cross to head towards the bridge, cross over on the road and walk back to your car.

🍴 **EATING AND DRINKING**

There's often an ice cream van in the car parks at Cadover Bridge and Shaugh Bridge. The Royal Oak at Meavy, a free house with good food and outdoor seating, is over 500 years old and is set on the village green near the 1,000-year-old tree from which it takes its name. The White Thorn pub at Shaugh Prior is another traditional hostelry, and welcomes families and dogs.

HILLSBOROUGH AND HELE BAY

Surprises at every turn on this stiff little coastal walk – including a haunted manor house.

Originally a market town and fishing port, the hilly town of Ilfracombe developed as a holiday resort in the mid-19th century, boosted by the coming of the London and South Western Railway in 1874. Ilfracombe is a real mix of faded grandeur and contemporary development, and is still a popular holiday resort. The harbour, overlooked by craggy cliffs and 15th-century St Nicholas Chapel on Lantern Hill – a landmark and votive chapel for fishermen and sailors – is particularly attractive, and seen at its best from Hillsborough (site of an Iron Age hill-fort) on this walk.

The tucked-away coves around Ilfracombe were home to illicit smuggling activity, as evidenced by the names of some: Brandy Cove, just west of Ilfracombe harbour, and Samson's Bay, to the east, where a man called Samson hid smuggled goods in a cave. Contraband may also have been stored at Chambercombe Manor.

Conservation Area

The North Devon Voluntary Marine Conservation Area extends for 15 miles (24km) from Hangman Point on the edge of Exmoor in the east to Woolacombe Sand in the west, including the section encountered on this walk, from the cliff base out to the 20m-depth contour. The rocky foreshores of this part of the coast, largely inaccessible on foot, are home to some of richest plant and animal communities in the country, situated where the colder North Atlantic waters meet warmer southern waters. Species include the wonderfully named snakelocks anenome and edible periwinkle.

An Industrial Past

The sheltered beach at Hele Bay, today overlooked by caravans, is the domain of the bucket-and-spade brigade. But 200 years ago the scene would have been different, when coal from South Wales was landed on the shore to feed the lime kilns that once sat at the back of the beach to produce fertiliser for local farmers. There are records of three ships still landing coal here from the start of the 20th century right up to the Second World War.

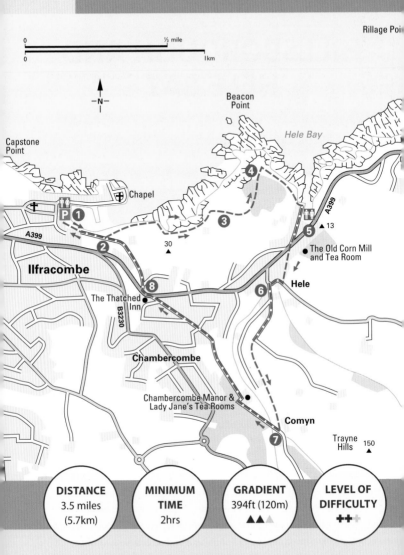

Rillage Poi

Beacon
Point

Hele Bay

Capstone
Point

Chapel

30

A399

A399

▲ 13

The Old Corn Mill
and Tea Room

Ilfracombe

Hele

The Thatched
Inn

B3230

Chambercombe

Chambercombe Manor &
Lady Jane's Tea Rooms

Comyn

Trayne
Hills   150
▲

½ mile

1km

—N—

DISTANCE	MINIMUM TIME	GRADIENT	LEVEL OF DIFFICULTY
3.5 miles (5.7km)	2hrs	394ft (120m) ▲▲▲	++ +

PATHS Undulating coast path, tracks, quiet lanes; steep and sometimes slippery
descent to Hele Bay **LANDSCAPE** Town, coast, wooded valley
SUGGESTED MAP OS Explorer 139 Bideford, Ilfracombe & Barnstaple
START/FINISH Grid reference: SS 523477
DOG FRIENDLINESS Under control at all times
PARKING Cove car park at Ilfracombe harbour (pay-and-display)
PUBLIC TOILETS Ilfracombe harbour and at Hele Bay

WALK 31 DIRECTIONS

❶ Walk along the right side of the harbour, soon passing through the Marine Drive car park. At the top exit, where the road narrows, bear left downhill on a path (note a small blue Coast Path sign on a lamppost).

❷ At a junction of paths follow Coast Path signs half left on a tarmac way. Where the path drops steeply ahead towards Rapparee Cove bear right up the left edge of a grassy area and climb steeply uphill, with a hedge left. Meet a fence at the top; bear left through a barrier and ascend through woodland. At the next junction turn right as signed (yellow arrow and acorn).

❸ At the next crosswords follow the Coast Path left up steps into Hillsborough Local Nature Reserve. Follow Coast Path signs, climbing steadily, soon with views inland over the Hele Valley. The path swings back towards the coast to reach a seat with excellent views.

❹ Keep following yellow arrows eventually to descend through woodland, turning sharp right downhill just before a viewpoint above Broadstrand Beach. Zig-zag downhill to reach the promenade at Hele Bay. Turn right, then right again up Beach Road to the A399.

❺ Cross over with care; head along a narrow wooded footpath to pass through the grounds of The Old Corn Mill and Tea Room, keeping ahead through a gate and up a narrow track to a lane. Turn right.

> ℗ **EATING AND DRINKING**
> This walk has plenty of opportunities for an ice cream or cup of tea. The Old Corn Mill and Tea Room, Hele Mill (seasonal) is a lovely spot, dating from the 16th century and rescued from dereliction in 1973. The mill and museum are open to the public. Lady Jane's Tea Rooms can be found at Chambercombe Manor (seasonal).

❻ Where the lane bears right keep straight ahead, signed to Comyn, soon turning left up a lane and climbing steadily. The lane reduces to a track; where it bears left keep ahead through a gate on a narrow hedged path, Cat Lane, to emerge through a gate by houses at Comyn. Turn right to reach a path junction.

❼ Turn right, signed 'Ilfracombe'. Pass Chambercombe Manor (open to the public and said to be haunted). The lane climbs gently out of this lovely hidden valley to meet a road on a bend among houses. Keep ahead and follow the road downhill to the A399.

❽ Cross over and turn left; turn first right opposite The Thatched Inn (an unusual building with outside seating) and follow the road to the Marine Drive car park and back to the harbour.

WEMBURY BEACH AND THE RIVER YEALM

Through fields to the wooded valley of the Yealm, with a return along the cliffs to the Marine Conservation Area.

The large parish of Wembury has an excellent network of well-maintained rights of way, giving all sorts of circular walk options. Our route affords fantastic views over South Devon's most beautiful estuary – the River Yealm, with views up Newton Creek, both popular with sailors – with a return along the Coast Path. And long-distance routes feature here too: the Devon Coast to Coast route – a combination of the Two Moors Way (102 miles/164km) and the Erme–Plym Trail (14 miles/22.5km) – meets the south coast at Wembury Beach.

Wembury Voluntary Marine Conservation Area

Wembury Beach is a great place for rock-pooling and spotting all manner of marine life. Information is available at the Marine Centre by the car park, open from Easter to the end of September (closed Mondays); entry is free, and a variety of seasonal events take place, such as beach cleans and rockshore rambles. The foreshore at Wembury Point was formed over 400 million years ago, and is part of a European Special Area of Conservation for its flora and fauna; several unusual species of fish, molluscs, worms and seaweeds have been recorded on the rocky reefs and wave-cut platforms.

St Werburgh's Church

The church is situated in a magical position above Blackstone Rocks and, unsurprisingly, the early 15th-century tower was used as a navigation landmark for sailors for hundreds of years. It is thought that the present church stands on the site of a Saxon oratory, dating possibly from the 9th century and replaced by a Norman church in the 12th century.

Waterside Villages

Make a day of it and take the ferry to Newton Ferrers or Noss Mayo, two delightfully picturesque waterside villages, both with good pubs. The ferry runs daily from Easter to the end of September from Warren Point to the Wide Slip at Noss Mayo, and Yealm Steps at Newton Ferrers.

Opposite: Rock overhang at Wembury Beach

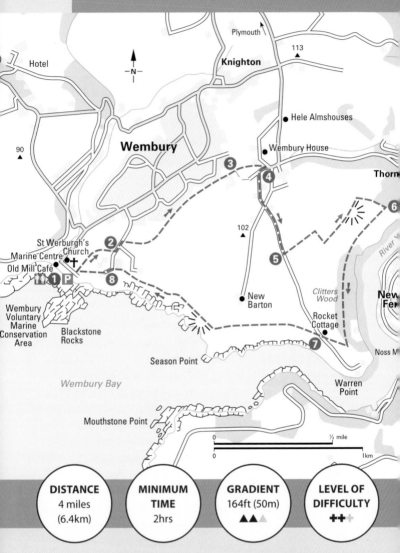

DISTANCE	MINIMUM TIME	GRADIENT	LEVEL OF DIFFICULTY
4 miles (6.4km)	2hrs	164ft (50m) ▲▲▲	++ +

PATHS Fields, tracks and woodland paths
LANDSCAPE Farmland, estuary, coast
SUGGESTED MAP OS Explorer OL20 South Devon
START/FINISH Grid reference: SX 518485
DOG FRIENDLINESS On lead in farmland (sheep on Coast Path)
PARKING National Trust car park, Wembury (fee, members free)
PUBLIC TOILETS Wembury beach

WALK 32 DIRECTIONS

1 Ascend steps near the car park entrance, by the honesty box. At the second Coast Path post turn left through a kissing gate. Follow the left edge of a meadow (for St Werburgh's Church turn left through a hedge gap) through a kissing gate on to a track.

2 Meet a lane; turn left and almost immediately right through a kissing gate into a field. Keep ahead and through a kissing gate; follow the left edge of two fields, then through a kissing gate onto a fenced path. The next gate meets a footpath T-junction on a green lane (Brownhill Lane).

3 Go straight ahead through a kissing gate; cross the field, aiming to the right of a high wall (the boundary to Wembury House, a late Georgian manor). Pass through a kissing gate on to a lane, with a green lane sharp right.

4 Turn right along the lane. Where it bears right towards New Barton Farm keep straight on through a gate on to National Trust land at Warren Point and follow a stony track, Warren Lane.

5 At a footpath sign turn left through a gate and along the top edge of the field. Turn right at the end, then left along a fenced section, and along the top edge of the next field to a footpath post. Turn right downhill towards the Yealm. Pass through two gates to meet a footpath junction.

6 Turn right to walk through Clitters Wood, eventually passing through a small gate above the Old Coastguard Station. A few paces later turn right up steps to a signpost and turn right, signed 'Wembury' (Warren Point/ferry left). This path reaches the Coast Path at a junction by Rocket Cottage.

🍴 EATING AND DRINKING

You can sit outside at The Old Mill Café at Wembury Beach (weekends only in winter) in a sheltered area at a table made out of an old millstone. Enjoy Fairtrade tea and coffee, good handmade pasties and cakes (wrapped for takeaway), and local crafts.

---

7 Follow the Coast Path ahead, soon passing through two kissing gates, and later another (Dartmoor ponies are used to preserve the clifftop maritime grassland here). At a fork keep left, with views to Cellar Beach. Drop across a stream; views open up to Wembury Point and Rame Head in Cornwall beyond. Pass through another kissing gate; eventually the path descends through another to leave National Trust land.

8 Pass a footpath, right. Where the track bears right inland, keep ahead on the Coast Path. At the next fork (the path ahead runs into the field by the church) bear left and follow the Coast Path to the starting point.

FREMINGTON QUAY AND THE TARKA TRAIL

Industrial history, a former railway line, diverse wildlife – there is masses to discover on this Taw estuary walk.

Scratch the surface at Fremington Quay and you'll discover all sorts of fascinating facts about this now tranquil spot. For centuries tidal Fremington Pill – navigable as far as the wonderfully named Muddlebridge Bridge, near the B3233 – was used by small vessels serving local needs. All that changed in the 19th century. By the late 1830s silting of the river prevented large cargo vessels from reaching Barnstaple, and so a deep-water quay was built at Fremington, with a horse-drawn line to Barnstaple, which later became part of the North Devon Railway. The coming of the railway boosted the fortunes of the quay considerably. Fremington Quay was at one time the busiest quay between Bristol and Land's End, exporting ball clay from Merton and Peters Marland, south of Fremington, and importing lime and coal from South Wales. The last cargo vessel to visit the quay was in 1969; the station had closed in 1968, although clay traffic continued until 1982.

The Tarka Trail
Today the old line has become part of the Tarka Trail, a 180-mile (290km) off-road cycle and walking route popular with all manner of cyclists, from families to long-distance users, following Sustrans National Cycle Route 3, known here as the West Country Way. This section of the Tarka Trail also forms part of the Devon Coast to Coast Cycle Route.

Flora and fauna
This part of the Taw estuary is characterised by large expanses of saltmarsh, an important wildlife habitat. Conservation work is carried out to preserve the saltmarsh by re-edging ditches to create a network of shallow channels and 'scrapes' (shallow depressions), which harbour hundreds of thousands of young fish and crabs – vital feeding grounds for birds. Oystercatchers and golden plover feed on the mudbanks and mussel beds, and the whole area is an internationally important wintering ground for migrant birds. The RSPB Isley Marsh reserve lies on the estuary at Yelland, just to the west of Fremington Quay.

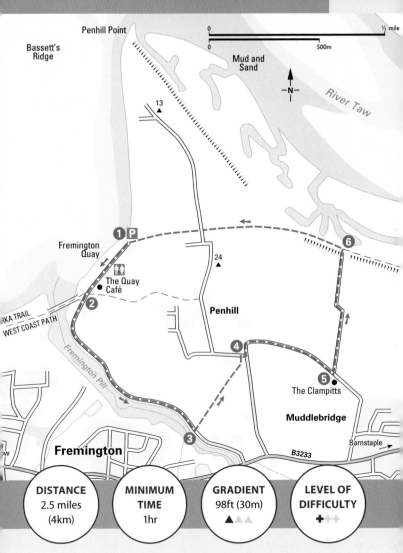

Mud and
Sand

River Taw

13

—N—

① P

Fremington
Quay

The Quay
Café

②

RKA TRAIL

WEST COAST PATH

Fremington Pill

24

Penhill

④

⑤ The Clampitts

Muddlebridge

③

Fremington

B3233

Barnstaple

DISTANCE	MINIMUM TIME	GRADIENT	LEVEL OF DIFFICULTY
2.5 miles (4km)	1hr	98ft (30m) ▲▲▲	✚✚✚

PATHS Lanes, field-edges, green lanes (some muddy after wet weather),
surfaced cycle track **LANDSCAPE** River estuary and creek
SUGGESTED MAP OS Explorer 139 Bideford, Ilfracombe & Barnstaple
START/FINISH Grid reference: SS 517335
DOG FRIENDLINESS On lead through farmland and lane
PARKING Fremington Quay car park (free)
PUBLIC TOILETS At Heritage Centre

WALK 33 DIRECTIONS

❶ Leave the car park via the approach road. On meeting the fenced picnic area (no dogs allowed) turn right along a concrete path that leads along the edge of the deepwater quay; look left to see the old signal box and station (now housing the Heritage Centre and the Quay Café) and remains of the platform; far ahead you'll see Saunton Down. As the bridge at the mouth of the pill is reached follow the path to meet the Tarka Trail, turn briefly right, then left to meet the lane.

> ### 🍴 EATING AND DRINKING
> The Quay Café is situated in the old station building; displays on the walls and in the Heritage Centre give details of local history and wildlife. Near by in Instow you'll find The Bar and The Wayfarer Inn, both near the waterfront.

❷ Turn right and follow the lane along Fremington Pill (note the 'walkers warning' sign and 15mph limit). This is a lovely stretch when the tide is in: look out for little egrets, which are commonly seen here. As the head of the pill comes into view look for a footpath signed left.

❸ Turn left over a non-dog-friendly stile or go through the gate. Follow the right edge of two fields, then along a short hedged grassy path (at times wet) to meet a lane.

❹ Turn right; where the lane bears sharp right by Penhill Cottage turn left on a bridleway along a hedged track on a public bridleway, which soon bears right. Follow it to a white house (Clampitt).

❺ Turn left on a footpath and go through a gate. The broad green lane descends gently, with expansive views over the River Taw. Kink left and right and descend to a tunnel under the old railway line (for stock to pass through). Cross a rough boardwalk over water, cross a stile, and mount steps on to the Tarka Trail.

❻ Turn left; the large expanse of saltmarsh towards the river is managed as a valuable wildlife habitat. The track passes through a cutting – look out for the meadow brown butterfly and blue field scabious – and under a huge railway bridge. At the end of the cutting, and where views over the estuary appear right, turn right on a small path to regain the car park.

> ### 🌿 IN THE AREA
> The Tarka Trail leads on to Barnstaple, the largest town in North Devon, which has a long history of seafaring: five ships joined the Armada fleet from the port in 1588. The Museum of Barnstaple and North Devon has excellent information on the area, and the Pannier Market and Butchers' Row in the heart of town will appeal to lovers of local food.

GREAT TORRINGTON AND THE RIVER TORRIDGE

Lepers, Conservators and Civil War skirmishes all play their part on this walk around Devon's 'Cavalier Town'.

The market town of Great Torrington, perched on a bluff overlooking a bend of the attractive River Torridge, is a fascinating place to visit, and this walk touches on a different historic period or event at every turn. It's worth noting that this short walk experiences a long descent at the start, and a correspondingly long climb back at the end – but the ascent in particular is steady and enjoys lovely views, and isn't as daunting as it may sound. A lovely level section leads along the banks of the River Torridge, which rises near the north Cornish coast and follows a curious route east before turning north to eventually join the Taw at Appledore.

The Cavalier Town

Visit the 'Torrington 1646' exhibition and you will be greeted by folk in period costume who will tell you everything you need to know about the town's fortunes during the English Civil War. The best way of understanding this bloody time is to pick up a copy of the Civil War Trail from the Information Centre. The town witnessed two important clashes in 1642 and 1643, and was the site of the last major battle of the war in February 1646 between more than 10,000 troops. The Royalists, who had barricaded the town, were finally driven out by Parliament's New Model Army under Sir Thomas Fairfax and Oliver Cromwell.

Along the Route

From the car park you get a very good view of two narrow strip fields on the other side of the valley. These two fields – once part of a group of seven – are known as the Lepers' Fields, worked by lepers living at the leper hospital in Taddiport in medieval times. Their earth hedgebanks have been restored and are maintained by traditional methods.

Look down the Torridge on Point ❷ for a glimpse of RHS Rosemoor Garden, open all year round. The walk also benefits from Torrington's 365 acres (148ha) of Common Land, given to the town in the 12th century and administered by 15 elected Conservators.

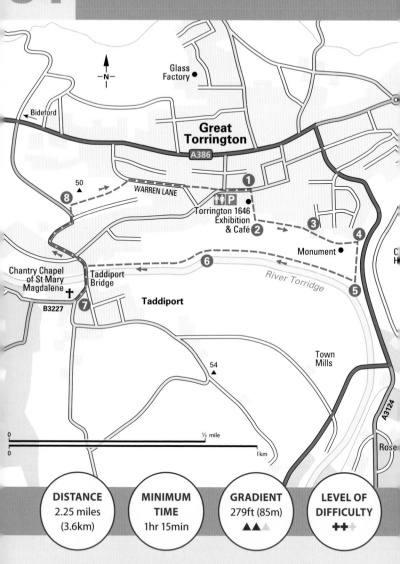

Great Torrington

A386

Glass Factory

← Bideford

50

WARREN LANE

8

Torrington 1646 Exhibition & Café

1

2

3

4

Monument

6

River Torridge

5

Chantry Chapel of St Mary Magdalene

Taddiport Bridge

Taddiport

7

B3227

54

Town Mills

A3124

Rose

0 ½ mile
0 1km

N

DISTANCE	MINIMUM TIME	GRADIENT	LEVEL OF DIFFICULTY
2.25 miles (3.6km)	1hr 15min	279ft (85m) ▲▲▲	++

PATHS Tarmac paths, woodland tracks, one steady descent/ascent, 1 stile

LANDSCAPE Riverside meadows, woodland, town

SUGGESTED MAP OS Explorer 126 Clovelly & Hartland

START/FINISH Grid reference: SS 495190

DOG FRIENDLINESS On lead through town

PARKING Castle Hill car park (pay-and-display)

PUBLIC TOILETS Castle Hill car park

WALK 34 DIRECTIONS

❶ Facing the steps to the TIC turn right and follow a wall through an archway in the far corner of the car park.

❷ Turn left on a tarmac path past high mid-19th-century castellated walls built by John, Lord Rolle. Pass another car park and a picnic area, with good views ahead towards Rosemoor Garden. The path (George's Path) starts to descend slightly.

❸ On meeting a grassy area with a seat ahead, turn right downhill, heading towards a stone obelisk commemorating the Battle of Waterloo (1815). At the monument turn left and follow a tarmac path downhill into woodland.

❹ The path bears right towards a road; as it does so turn right down steps, and follow the broad path (Lady Wash) downhill to meet a track on the bank of the River Torridge.

❺ Turn right on this broad track under lofty oaks (particularly lovely in spring and autumn) on the former Rolle Canal, opened in 1827 to improve transport links from the coast inland. This section was filled in and became a toll road, while part of its course was sold to the London and South Western Railway, which reached Great Torrington in 1872. At a gate ahead turn left down steps on to a narrow path close to the river. Where the river curves away left keep ahead through a barrier on to the track.

❻ Immediately turn left onto Ladies Island. Keep along the left edge to regain the river then follow it to cross a stile onto the road by Taddiport Bridge.

❼ To visit Chantry Chapel of the Leper Hospital of St Mary Magdalene, turn left over the bridge and follow the road; the chapel is on the right. Retrace your steps over the bridge and follow the road, bearing left past the Torridge Inn (closed at the time of writing) and disused milk factory. Ascend Limers Hill to enter the Commons.

❽ At the second footpath sign (right) turn right and take the left (higher) of two paths, climbing steadily to reach Warren Lane. Turn right: where the lane bears right downhill keep ahead through railings into Rack Park, so-named from the days when fleeces and woven cloth were laid on racks to dry in the sun. Exit the park on to Mill Street; cross into South Street and keep ahead to find the car park.

🍴 EATING AND DRINKING

There are pubs and cafés in town – try the Black Horse Inn on the High Street, believed to date from the 15th century and headquarters to both Royalists and Parliamentarians at different times during the Civil War. There's also a café and garden in the Torrington 1646 exhibition on the car park.

THE DEVIL VERSUS THE CHURCH

A walk around North Brentor on Dartmoor's western edge in the shadow of the Church of St Michael de Rupe.

Anyone exploring western Dartmoor cannot fail to notice a conical peak, topped with a tower, protruding high above the rolling fields and woodlands towards the Cornish border. This strange natural formation is Brent Tor and, surprisingly, has nothing to do with the granite tors of Dartmoor. It is a remnant of the mass of lava that poured out on to the seabed here more than 300 million years ago, when the area was a shallow sea. The softer rocks around have been eroded away over the millennia, leaving behind this extraordinary landmark 1,100ft (335m) above sea level. The hill overlooks peaceful North Brentor village, where the walk starts; an optional extension visits the Church of St Michael de Rupe.

A Spectacular Location

The 13th-century Church of St Michael de Rupe ('of the rock') was originally built by Robert Giffard, Lord of the Manor of Lamerton and Whitchurch, in c1130. Rebuilt towards the end of the 13th century, the 40ft (12.2m) tower was added during the 15th century. The views from here are quite breathtaking.

It is said that while the church was being built the Devil hurled stones from the top of the hill on to the unfortunate parishioners below. Another legend tells of how a wealthy 14th-century merchant vowed to build a church here in gratitude to St Michael – the patron saint of seamen – for saving him and his ship from a storm at sea. The Devil destroyed the building work every night, so the merchant called on St Michael to help again. The saint chased the Devil away and in return the church was dedicated to St Michael.

North Brentor was added to the parish in 1880, and all burials then took place at Christ Church in the village, since the soil on top of Brent Tor was too thin to accommodate a decent grave. Burial logistics seem to have featured strongly in this part of Devon over the years. The Church of St Petroc at Lydford, originally a Saxon foundation, used to hold the only consecrated ground close to the northern part of the moor. Bodies were carried across the moor for burial along a route known as the Lich Way.

Opposite: Church of St Michael de Rupe, Brent Tor

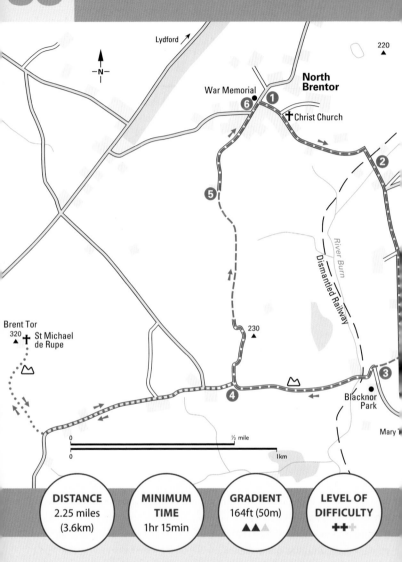

DISTANCE
2.25 miles
(3.6km)

MINIMUM TIME
1hr 15min

GRADIENT
164ft (50m)
▲▲△

LEVEL OF DIFFICULTY
╋╋╋

PATHS Tracks and paths (some muddy after wet weather), fields, quiet lanes; steep climb to church (optional) **LANDSCAPE** Farmland, open moorland

SUGGESTED MAP OS Explorer 112 Launceston & Holsworthy

START/FINISH Grid reference: SX 481815

DOG FRIENDLINESS On lead in farmland and edge of Gibbet Hill

PARKING Laneside parking near war memorial in North Brentor

PUBLIC TOILETS None on route

WALK 35 DIRECTIONS

❶ The walk starts from the war memorial in the centre of North Brentor. Walk down Station Road to pass the phone box, church and village hall. Follow the lane as it bears right to cross the former London and South Western railway line, which operated from 1890 to 1960. You can see the old station below you to the right.

❷ Pass over the cattle grid on to the moor, and up the lane to pass a line of beech trees in the wall right, and the entrance to Wortha Farm. Where the granite wall on the right comes close to the lane bear right to follow it downhill to meet a lane.

❸ Turn right and walk gently downhill to pass Blacknor Park (left), then a cattle grid. The lane becomes rocky and drops steeply to pass Wortha Mill, then crosses the disused railway line and the River Burn. The track ascends steeply to a T-junction. For the optional extension to St Michael's turn left to pass South Brentor Farm to a lane junction on a U-bend; keep ahead (left), later slightly uphill to pass Hillside and later Coles Cottage. Pass Brennen Cottage; a few paces later the lane bends sharp left. Turn right through a gate and keep ahead up the right edge of the field on a permitted path. At the top turn right through a gate, later bearing left and climbing steeply to the church.

❹ On the main route turn right on a public footpath along a hedged track, which leads to two gates. Pass through the right-hand one as signed and keep straight ahead to pass a footpath post to the right of a pond. Pick your way over an area of bumpy ground to descend to a stile into a damp field, with wonderful views towards Gibbet Hill right. Bear diagonally right across the field, aiming towards North Brentor church. Pass through a kissing gate, in the next field head across to pass through a hedge gap next to a kissing gate. Keep across the next field, with a hedgebank left, aiming for a gate.

❺ Follow footpath signs down a narrow hedged path, muddy after wet weather. The path broadens to a track to meet Darke Lane, keep ahead to a T-junction.

❻ Turn right to the war memorial and the start.

🍴 EATING AND DRINKING

The unusually named Elephant's Nest at Horndon, a small hamlet just east of Mary Tavy, serves excellent food and drink and has a very pretty garden. The Mary Tavy Inn is found on the A386 at Mary Tavy, and a couple of miles north, the 16th-century Castle Inn at Lydford is worth a visit. There is also a National Trust restaurant at Lydford Gorge.

NORTHAM BURROWS COUNTRY PARK

Pick a calm day for this walk around a peninsula of coastal grassland, with views across the broad Taw–Torridge estuary.

Northam Burrows, a Site of Special Scientific Interest, is an extraordinary and unexpected feature on the more usually rugged North Devon coast: 625 acres (253ha) of level, windswept, grassy coastal plain jutting out into the Taw–Torridge estuary, fringed by sand dunes, tidal mudflats and saltmarsh, the haunt of sheep, horses and wading birds. The route suggested follows the Coast Path round the rim of the country park, and returns across the neck of the peninsula, weaving around the golf club greens (fenced off to protect them from livestock).

Along the way, look across the estuary to the high sand dunes of Braunton Burrows, designated (with the estuary, Northam Burrows and Braunton Marsh) the UK's first UNESCO Biosphere Reserve in 2002 on account of its unique flora and fauna; over 500 species of flowering plant have been identified. Braunton's Great Field is a rare example of a medieval field system.

Flora and Fauna
The Burrows are made up of a number of varied habitats, each supporting different flora and fauna. The dunes behind the pebble ridge run along the north-western side of the Burrows, and separate the Atlantic from the coastal grassland. On the fixed dunes (behind the mobile windblown ones nearer the shore) badgers and rabbits may be seen, and ground-nesting birds such as wheatear and skylark. The grassland areas are grazed by sheep and horses and criss-crossed by 15 miles (24km) of drainage ditches. Skern, passed on Point 3, is an area of mudflat colonised by saltmarsh, a feeding ground for waders and wintering birds such as Brent geese.

Westward Ho!
The village of Westward Ho! (from where the Pebblridge car park is accessed) is a strange mix of large Victorian houses, static caravan parks and contemporary apartment blocks. The settlement developed post-1855 after the publication of *Westward Ho!*, a novel by Charles Kingsley (1819–75) who spent his childhood at Clovelly (see Walk 39), a few miles west along the coast.

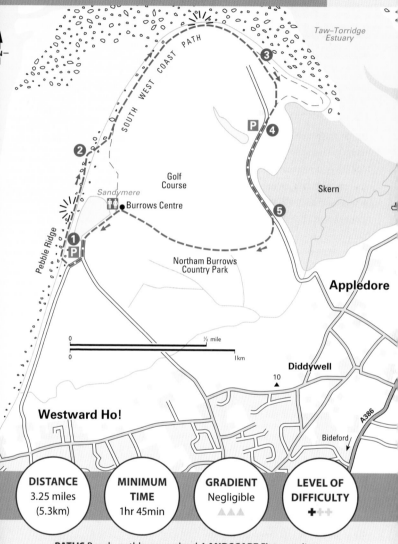

| DISTANCE 3.25 miles (5.3km) | MINIMUM TIME 1hr 45min | GRADIENT Negligible ▲▲▲ | LEVEL OF DIFFICULTY +++ |

PATHS Beach, pathless grassland **LANDSCAPE** Flat coastline
SUGGESTED MAP OS Explorer 139 Bideford, Ilfracombe & Barnstaple
START/FINISH Grid reference: SS 438305 **DOG FRIENDLINESS** Under control
at all times: livestock and wildlife; no dogs on beach 1 May–end September
PARKING Pebbleridge car park (free) **PUBLIC TOILETS** The Burrows Centre (when
open) and at top of slip at Westward Ho! **NOTE** Gates to the Country Park shut
6pm–7am winter, 10pm–7am summer; small entrance fee for cars in summer; do
not walk on the estuarine tidal mudflats

WALK 36 DIRECTIONS

❶ From the car park there is a choice of two routes. You can cross the walkway over the pebble ridge by the information board, and turn right along the 2-mile (3.2km) long Westward Ho! beach, passing low dunes, with views towards Lundy (left). Past low sandy cliffs the ridge bears right; look for a gap in the dunes, beyond which you will see a Coast Path post. Alternatively, follow Coast Path signs along the track past Sandymere (a seasonal pool), then between the dunes and Burrows Centre, to reach the post. The centre is open from the end of May to early September; toilets accessible from Easter to the end of October.

🕭 EATING AND DRINKING

The Pebbleridge Café at the Northam entrance to the country park is open all year round and has drinking water for dogs. The friendly and comfortable Village Inn is reputed to be the oldest building in Westward Ho! dating from 1750 when it was a farm, and serves good home-made food.

---

❷ Bear right across the pebble ridge to the Coast Path post, and continue along the edge of the Burrows, following yellow arrows past the 8th hole of the Royal North Devon Golf Club and along the Taw–Torridge estuary, with views to Braunton Burrows. Cross a level grassy area, with

---

🕮 IN THE AREA

Appledore – a trading and fishing village since the 14th century – on the banks of the Torridge is a wonderful mix of narrow lanes and drangs (alleyways), old fisherman's cottages, and artists' studios. Long famous for boatbuilding, Appledore's shipyard is still active today. A passenger ferry crosses the Torridge to Instow.

---

views ahead to Appledore and Instow on the opposite bank of the Torridge.

❸ Eventually look right to see a line of seats overlooking Skern tidal marsh overlooked by a small parking area; bear right at this point across level grassland, aiming for the parking area.

❹ Pass to the left of the car park, and follow the access lane along the edge of Skern, a magnet for birdlife on account of its rich food supply. The best time to spot waders is one to two hours before high tide.

❺ At the first 'sleeping policeman' turn right down a grassy bank, keeping to the left of a broad grassy sward. Initially head for the cliffs to the west of Westward Ho! then straighten up, soon aiming for the Burrows Centre. Eventually bear right to pass hole 15 and meet a gravelly track, which bears to the left of the centre. Follow the track past the mere to the car park.

BAGGY POINT AND CROYDE BAY

Magnificent coastal scenery, far-reaching views,
wild flowers, seabirds and seals – a North Devon classic.

For those unused to the South West Coast Path this walk makes a good introduction, in that the path is relatively easy and the views exceptional. There are plenty of opportunities for walks in this area, but this route to Baggy Point is one of the best.

Baggy Point

Baggy Point is within the North Devon Area of Outstanding Natural Beauty, and the coastal scenery here is truly magnificent. The Devonian rocks date back 370 million years, and the rugged cliffs – comprising sandstone, shale, slate and limestone – rise in places to about 200ft (61m). In 1799 HMS *Weazle* was driven on to rocks off the end of Baggy Point, with the loss of all 106 lives on board.

Keep an eye out for grey Atlantic seals in the waters off Baggy Point. Lundy Island is home to a breeding population of around 60, and seals seen off the North Devon coast in summer return to Lundy to breed in winter. Britain is home to over three-quarters of Europe's grey seal population.

The point's hard sandstone faces are a popular seacliff climbing venue, comprising three main collections of south-facing slabs – you may see climbers as you approach the gate on Point ❹. The many climbing routes rejoice in such wonderful names such as Scrattling Zawn, Kinky Cowboy, Twinkletoes and – possible less appealing – Death on a Stick.

Henry Williamson

As you pass through the gate at Point ❸ you will see an inscription to the North Devon writer Henry Williamson (1895–1977), who took his inspiration from the Devon coast and countryside. He rented a cottage in Georgeham – just inland from Croyde – in 1921, and moved with his family to South Molton in 1929. Williamson's most famous novel, *Tarka the Otter* – the story of the life and death of an otter, born on the River Torridge – was published in 1927. Williamson wrote extensively about local nature and countryside, and produced over 50 titles.

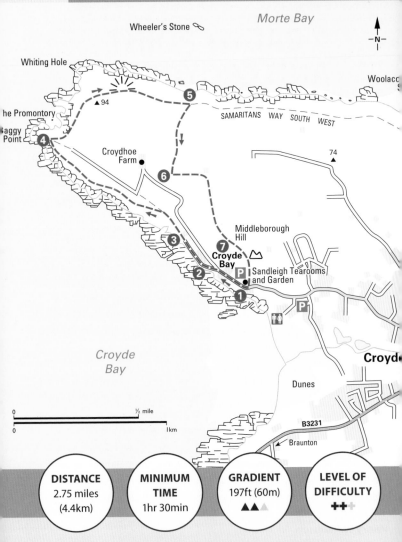

Morte Bay

Wheeler's Stone

Whiting Hole

he Promontory

aggy Point

Woolacc

5

SAMARITANS WAY SOUTH WEST

▲ 94

Croydhoe Farm

4

6

▲ 74

Middleborough Hill

3

7

Croyde Bay

2

P

Sandleigh Tearooms and Garden

1

Croyd

Croyde Bay

Dunes

0   ½ mile

0   1km

B3231

Braunton

DISTANCE	MINIMUM TIME	GRADIENT	LEVEL OF DIFFICULTY
2.75 miles (4.4km)	1hr 30min	197ft (60m) ▲▲▲	++ +

PATHS Good coastal footpath, fields, steep descent to finish, 4 stiles

LANDSCAPE Coast and farmland

SUGGESTED MAP OS Explorer 139 Bideford, Ilfracombe & Barnstaple

START/FINISH Grid reference: SS 432397

DOG FRIENDLINESS On lead through National Trust farmland

PARKING National Trust Baggy Point car park (seasonal/members free),
Croyde Bay **PUBLIC TOILETS** At Croyde Sand

WALK 37 DIRECTIONS

1 From the car park turn right along the lane, signed 'Baggy Point', between houses, soon passing through stone gateposts onto the cliffs. Follow the tarmac way past the entrance to Croyde Hoy Farm, and past houses behind shelter belts of tamarisk.

2 Where the tarmac way leads towards a contemporary building, bear slightly left on the Coast Path to pass a big chunk of whalebone, washed up on the beach in 1915.

3 Pass a small wildlife pond built by the Hyde family – who gave Baggy Point to the National Trust in 1939 – through a gate. Reach a footpath junction and keep ahead on the Coast Path, soon passing steps right down to the beach and rockpools below. This easy stretch of Coast Path ascends gently towards vertical cliffs off Baggy Point. Look out for wild flowers in spring and summer: pink thrift, blue scabious, white bladder campion, yellow tormentil and honeysuckle.

4 Follow the path sharp right (or keep ahead on to The Promontory) and through a gate, overlooking dramatic Slab Cove. Turn left beside the wire fence; keep ahead to pass a rocket pole, used in life-saving exercises. Meet a wall corner and continue, with the wall right, with fabulous views to Morte Point and 3-mile (4.8km) long Woolacombe

Sand, backed by dunes. At the end of the wall pass through a gate.

5 Reach a path junction by a bench and bear right, signed to the car park. Pass over a stile and keep ahead uphill, with a hedgebank left. Crest the hilltop; drop gently to cross a stile and continue in the same direction.

> 🍴 **EATING AND DRINKING**
> Right next to the car park, tucked away in a lovely sheltered, walled garden, you will find Sandleigh Tearooms and Garden. Run in conjunction with the National Trust, the refreshments on offer are augmented by a number of flourishing organic raised vegetable beds (local allotments). Open daily from March to November, and winter weekends.

6 When level with Croyde Hoe Farm (right) turn left over a stile, and along the top left edge of the field. Turn right at the end and drop to pass through a gate at the head of a small combe. Continue uphill; where the wall left ends keep ahead to the top of Middleborough Hill.

7 Bear left past a bench, and continue left round the viewpoint to a footpath post. Keep ahead on a narrow path that descends steeply through gorse to pass through a kissing gate, and then another into a field. Head downhill, aiming for a stile at the left end of the car park.

WHERE TAMAR AND TAVY MEET

A look at the fascinating industrial history and internationally important birdlife of Devon's most hidden corner.

Two of South Devon's greatest rivers, the Tavy and the Tamar, meet just south of the pretty little peninsula village of Bere Ferrers. This is one of the most picturesque locations in the county and with just 1.5 miles (2.4km) of land joining the peninsula from the rest of Devon you do feel that you are surrounded by water on all sides. The Tamar here forms the Devon–Cornwall boundary.

Today, the Tamar estuaries are an internationally important wildlife habitat due to their mixture of ancient oak woodlands, saltmarsh and rocky foreshore. Huge populations of birds overwinter here or drop in during migration. Look out for common and green sandpipers on the Tavy, and the striking white little egret (like a small heron), that roosts in the trees and feeds on small fish and crustaceans.

A Vital Lifeline

These rivers have witnessed a huge amount of activity over the generations. Remnants of fords, quays and crossing places can be seen on both the Tamar and Tavy, dating from a time when most transport of people and goods was by water rather than overland.

The area's prosperity came from the many silver and lead mines, active from the 13th to 16th centuries, and again in the 19th. Silver and lead were exported downriver to Plymouth; coal from South Wales and lime came back up again. In the early 19th century more than 1,000 people were employed in local mines, the main ones being South Hooe Mine and South Tamar Consols. Weir Quay, on the west side of the peninsula, was the main quay for the import and export of goods. There are remains of lime kilns on both rivers, where lime was burned to produce fertiliser.

Another important local product was fruit; the valleys enjoy a particularly balmy climate. There are records of black cherries, pears, strawberries and walnuts being produced and exported in the late 18th century. The coming of the railway in 1890 greatly assisted the fruit and flower growers as their produce could reach markets more quickly; daffodils are still grown locally.

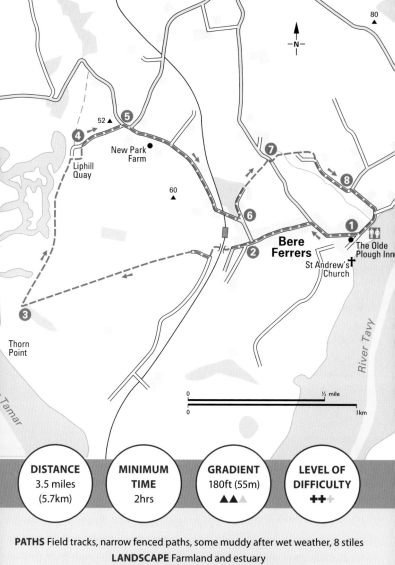

WALK 38 DIRECTIONS

1 From the war memorial and well (1852) walk uphill away from the river; note St Andrew's Church left. By the Social Club turn left into Station Road, passing the church hall.

2 Where the lane bears right keep ahead up a lane ('Station Road') and pass under the railway line. Keep ahead up a track, bearing left over a stile by a gate, and across the field. Pass through a small gate in a larger one and continue, with a fence left, eventually descending with glorious views over the River Tamar into Cornwall; look right to see the Tamar and Royal Albert bridges in Plymouth.

3 Turn right along the bottom of the field, with beautiful oaks left and reed beds beyond. Bear right at the end, then left over a V-stile, through a gate and along boardwalks; the path returns to the river. Pass through a gate (access to water, left); follow the fenced path to a junction. Turn right uphill, then left over a stile and descend steeply behind a house; cross a ladder stile onto a track at Liphill Quay, a one-time smuggling spot.

4 Turn right; the track climbs steeply to meet a lane. Look back for views over the saltmarsh, an important wildlife habitat.

5 Turn right to pass Ormonde House; continue downhill to cross the railway and station.

6 Just past the station turn left down a drive (concealed footpath sign), soon passing through the left of two gateways (The Coach House) into the grounds of The Old Rectory. As the drive bears right towards the house keep ahead across the garden, bearing right at the hedge. Turn left through a gate; follow a fenced path down across the field to cross a stile onto a lane. Turn right for a few paces.

7 Turn left over a ladder stile. Head across boggy ground and ascend rough grassland to a footpath post; turn right over a stile on a narrow path. Cross a stile and keep along the right edge of the field. Turn right at the end through a gate; head downhill, passing the entrance to Shutecombe, to meet a lane on a bend.

8 Keep ahead; the lane meets the Tavy foreshore and bears right past the harbour. Follow Fore Street uphill past The Olde Plough Inn to the start point.

🍴 EATING AND DRINKING

You won't want to leave this magical spot so look no further than The Olde Plough Inn in Fore Street: there's been an inn here for over 400 years. Good home-cooked food – using local suppliers wherever possible, and fresh fish a speciality – live music and theme nights, and a beer garden with views to the Tavy, all add to its appeal.

BUCK'S MILLS AND WORTHYGATE WOOD

A tough route along wooded cliffs above
the remote former fishing hamlet of Buck's Mills.

Much of the 11.25-mile (18km) stretch of South West Coast Path between Westward Ho! and Clovelly on Devon's north coast is clothed with pretty oak woodland, and this walk explores delightful Worthygate Wood to the east of the little hamlet of Buck's Mills, the only settlement encountered on the route. Visitors to the tourist hot spot of Clovelly further west, an old fishing village that clings to the steep cliffs above a 14th-century quay, may be surprised at the contrast with Buck's Mills, today simply a collection of white-painted cottages above a rocky beach. But those seeking peace and quiet may well prefer it, and enjoy exploring the lovely Woodland Trust woods that clothe the steep-sided valleys above the hamlet, awash with wild daffodils in March and bluebells in May.

Buck's Mills was always a close-knit community: a fishing village with its own quay and lime kilns, and remarkably self-sufficient. In days gone by some of the inhabitants travelled across the waters to Lundy Island to work in the granite quarries there.

A Local Benefactress

Prior to the consecration of St Anne's Church – which sits shrouded in trees half-way up the valley – the inhabitants of Buck's Mills had to carry their dead inland to Parkham or Woolfardisworthy along a route that became known as the 'Coffin Road'. In 1860 the philanthropic Mrs Jane Marianne Elwes had a house built here, and sponsored the construction of the church. Old notice boards found inside record the fact that 140 seats were to be retained 'for free and exclusive use of the poor forever'.

Local Wildlife

You probably won't be lucky enough to spot roe deer in the ancient broadleaved woodlands around Buck's Mills. This shy species – most active at dawn and dusk – was widespread in the Middle Ages, but disappeared and was reintroduced in the late 19th century. Look out for the white rump patch, which fluffs out when the animal is alarmed.

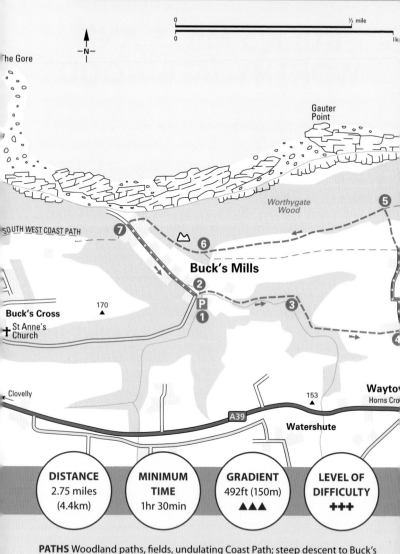

The Gore

Gauter Point

Worthygate Wood

SOUTH WEST COAST PATH

Buck's Mills

Buck's Cross
St Anne's Church

Clovelly

Wayto
Horns Cro

A39

Watershute

½ mile

1k

DISTANCE 2.75 miles (4.4km)	MINIMUM TIME 1hr 30min	GRADIENT 492ft (150m) ▲▲▲	LEVEL OF DIFFICULTY +++

PATHS Woodland paths, fields, undulating Coast Path; steep descent to Buck's Mills, 3 stiles **LANDSCAPE** Wooded valley, farmland, wooded coast

SUGGESTED MAP OS Explorer 126 Clovelly & Hartland

START/FINISH Grid reference: SS 358233

DOG FRIENDLINESS On lead through farmland

PARKING Car park above Buck's Mills (free)

PUBLIC TOILETS None on route

WALK 39 DIRECTIONS

❶ From the bottom left corner of the car park take a narrow path to meet the lane on a corner.

❷ Ignore a small footpath sharp right and instead turn 90 degrees right on a footpath to cross the stream on a railed footbridge and pass behind a sadly derelict cottage. The path – the Coffin Road – ascends through ancient broadleaved woodland, following the stream. The Woodland Trust is gradually clearing stands of planted Sitka spruce and larch to encourage regeneration of broadleaved species.

❸ Cross a tributary on a wooden plank, then ascend more steeply out of the valley and through a gate into a field. Follow the right edge; pass by a stile, go through a small gate at the end of a barn. Cross the yard at Lower Worthygate and through a gate, then pass the farmhouse to a footpath junction.

❹ Turn left up the drive to meet a lane; turn left to pass Higher Worthygate. Where the lane bears sharp right turn left on a footpath; after a few paces turn right over a stile on to an uneven and rocky hedged path, signed to the Coast Path. Cross two stiles and descend past the overgrown Gauter Pool (left) to meet the Coast Path.

❺ Turn left along the narrow and at times slippery and muddy path through oak woodland (Worthygate Wood). This undulating path eventually emerges into grass and bracken before re-entering woodland and dropping to a path junction.

> 🍴 **EATING AND DRINKING**
> Try The Hoops Inn on the A39 at Horns Cross (there has been a hostelry here since the 13th century) for good fish and local meat, or The Bell Inn at Parkham.

❻ Turn right to descend steeply, at times rockily underfoot, eventually zig-zagging downhill and descending steps to reach the lane amongst a cluster of white cottages at Buck's Mills.

❼ Turn left and follow the lane uphill; as it bears right keep ahead up the narrow path to regain the car park.

> 🌿 **IN THE AREA**
> For a completely different experience take a trip to Clovelly. There's an entrance charge, and this once tranquil spot is today thronged with visitors. Donkeys used to transport goods up and down the steep narrow cobbled street to the quay. The novelist Charles Kingsley, author of *Westward Ho!* and *The Water Babies* (see Walk 36), lived here when his father was rector of the church.

BLACKPOOL MILL AND HARTLAND QUAY

A surprisingly easy walk along a section of the toughest stretch of the South West Coast Path.

That part of North Devon lying east of the A39 Bude to Bideford road is often ignored by tourist guides, and little explored – and that's exactly why it is so wonderful. This easy walk from the nearby hamlet of Stoke touches on what is undoubtedly the most strenuous section of the South West Coast Path, but only includes one lengthy steep ascent – and the views more than make up for any pain.

Hartland Point

Devon's north-west tip is characterised by an extraordinary change in the nature of the coast. The cliffs along the coast from Clovelly, to the east, although high, are relatively calm and flat-topped, yet turn the corner at Hartland lighthouse and you enter a different world, where the craggy rocks on the seabed run in jagged parallel lines towards the unforgiving cliffs. The Coast Path to the south of the point traverses over what is, in effect, a mass of vertical tiltings and contortions, caused by lateral pressure on the earth's crust around 300 million years ago.

Extraordinary Hartland Quay dates back to 1586, when its building was authorised by Act of Parliament. Cargoes of coal, lime and timber were landed here, and in 1616 lead was brought in for repairs to the roof of St Nectan's Church at Stoke. The quay was active until 1893, and once abandoned was soon destroyed by the ravages of the sea. The buildings, including stables for the donkeys that carried goods up the cliff, have now been converted into the Hartland Quay Hotel, museum and shop.

Lundy Island

The island of Lundy, famous for its puffins (the first pair to breed for many years was recorded in 2005) is a granite outcrop best seen from the cliffs near the lighthouse. You can take a boat from either Bideford or Ilfracombe, on a day trip, or a helicopter from Hartland Point. Every journey to the island is tinged with the added edge that the weather conditions might not let you get there at all – or, of course, get home again quite when you planned.

Opposite: St Catherine's Tor rises up beyond Hartland Quay

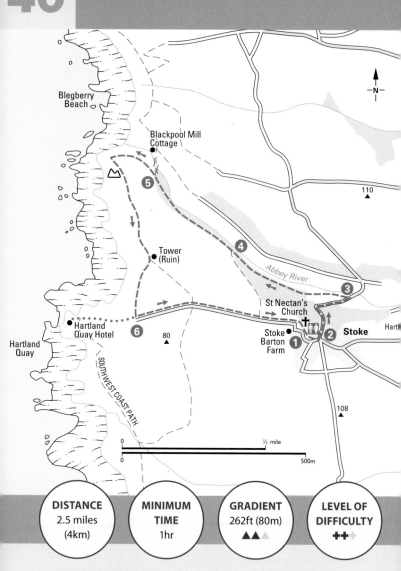

DISTANCE	MINIMUM TIME	GRADIENT	LEVEL OF DIFFICULTY
2.5 miles (4km)	1hr	262ft (80m) ▲▲△	++✚

PATHS Woodland tracks (some muddy after weather), Coast Path, fields 3 stiles
LANDSCAPE Wooded valley, rugged coastline and farmland
SUGGESTED MAP OS Explorer 126 Clovelly & Hartland
START/FINISH Grid reference: SS 239247 **DOG FRIENDLINESS** On lead on
Coast Path and in farmland **PARKING** Laneside near St Nectan's Church, Stoke
(not in church car park) **PUBLIC TOILETS** Stoke village **NOTE** Do not attempt
this walk in very strong winds or coastal fog; do not approach the cliff edge

WALK 40 DIRECTIONS

❶ The walk starts from the gates to 14th-century St Nectan's Church at Stoke. Walk towards the church; at the south door turn right to leave the churchyard through the lychgate.

❷ Immediately past the toilets turn left down a steep and deeply banked lane (unsuitable for vehicles), dropping into the valley of the Abbey River. At the bottom look right across a pond and parkland to see Hartland Abbey.

❸ Turn left through a gate at a footpath to Coast Path sign, and walk through a rough field. Go through a gate (very muddy) into woodland, and follow the track down the valley, soon descending to run along the river. Where a small path descends right to the riverbank keep on the upper path to pass into a field and meet a junction.

❹ Keep straight on, soon passing back into woodland with glimpses of the sea ahead. The river below passes through a small gorge.

⌀ IN THE AREA

Hartland Abbey, passed on Point **❷**, and dating from 1157, was a monastery for 400 years and has been a family home since 1539. The delightful gardens – designed by Gertrude Jekyll — and grounds benefit from its sheltered location, just 1 mile (1.6km) from some of the most stunning coastal scenery in the country.

❺ Meet the Coast Path, with a bridge over the river right. Bear left and through a gate; continue through blackthorn towards open ground, with views over rocky Blegberry Beach ahead (accessed by turning right over the bridge). At the Coast Path sign above the beach bear left and climb very steeply uphill. The path levels off and continues along the top of massive cliffs (do not go near the edge) to pass the remains of 18th-century Pleasure House, with views right over Hartland Quay. Keep ahead, aiming for a stile to the left of the Rocket House, built in the 1890s, ahead.

🍴 EATING AND DRINKING

The Hartland Quay Hotel can be reached on foot or by car (small toll charge in season). Hartland has a range of pubs, and Hartland Farm Shop has a café and local produce. You can also get fish and chips in the square. Excellent cream teas are available (seasonal) at Stoke Barton Farm, Stoke.

❻ For Hartland Quay and hotel pass to the right of the Rocket House and follow the Coast Path steeply downhill. Turn left inside the field and follow the hedgebank; cross a stile and continue. Pass through a small gate and follow a narrow path with houses left, crossing a stile en route. Cross the stile in the church wall, and bear right through the churchyard to the start point.

Walking in Safety

All these walks are suitable for any reasonably fit person, but less experienced walkers should try the easier walks first. Route finding is usually straightforward, but you will find that an Ordnance Survey map is a useful addition to the route maps and descriptions.

RISKS

Although each walk here has been researched with a view to minimising the risks to the walkers who follow its route, no walk in the countryside can be considered to be completely free from risk. Walking in the outdoors will always require a degree of common sense and judgement to ensure that it is as safe as possible.

- Be particularly careful on cliff paths and in upland terrain, where the consequences of a slip can be very serious.
- Remember to check tidal conditions before walking on the seashore.
- Some sections of route are by, or cross, busy roads. Take care and remember traffic is a danger even on minor country lanes.
- Be careful around farmyard machinery and livestock, especially if you have children with you.
- Be aware of the consequences of changes in the weather and check the forecast before you set out. Carry spare clothing and a torch if you are walking in the winter months. Remember the weather can change very quickly at any time of the year, and in moorland and heathland areas, mist and fog can make route finding much harder. Don't set out in these conditions unless you are confident of your navigation skills in poor visibility. In summer remember to take account of the heat and sun; wear a hat and carry spare water.

On walks away from centres of population you should carry a whistle and survival bag. If you do have an accident requiring the emergency services, make a note of your position as accurately as possible and dial 999.

COUNTRYSIDE CODE

- Be safe, plan ahead and follow any signs.
- Leave gates and property as you find them.
- Protect plants and animals and take your litter home.
- Keep dogs under close control.
- Consider other people.

For more information on the Countryside Code visit:
www.naturalengland.org.uk/ourwork/enjoying/countrysidecode